Praise for BAREFOOT REVOLUTION

In our contemporary Christian world, many voices claim the secret of a vibrant spiritual life. Paul Marshall boldly walks right into this zone. This is a book about a living, serious, disciplined *relationship* with God that calls us out of materialism, shallowness, and passivity. If you are hungry for something deeper, for "grown up" rather than "adolescent" spirituality and are willing to be challenged and examined, then this book is for you.
  –Derek Morphew, Academic Dean of the Vineyard Institute
  and author of *Breakthrough: Discovering the Kingdom*

In *Barefoot Revolution*, Paul encourages us to walk through life "barefoot"—available and ready for God—resulting in a life marked by both spiritual power and radical love. Exposing the counterfeits, Paul shows how to live a genuine life with God by finding a rhythm rather than merely following the rules. An inspiring and helpful book.
  –Mark Fields, Director of Global and Intercultural Ministry for Vineyard USA

Barefoot Revolution is a plucky, ruthlessly practical exposition of how to move from dry flatlands of spirituality to burning bush experiences fueled by God's love. Paul Marshall, a missional pastor who has caringly washed people's feet for two decades in one of Australia's most ravaged cities, forges his words to bring about dynamic transformation for those desirous of finding God and blessing their neighbors.
  –Robert L. Gallagher, PhD, Associate Professor of Intercultural Studies,
  Wheaton College Graduate School

Barefoot Revolution is a powerful book that covers the very basic tenets of Christianity in an encouraging yet challenging way. I can't stress enough how important this book is for both new Christians and seasoned saints (and everyone in between).
  –Kathi Macias, writer, speaker, and author of *The 40 Day Devotional Challenge* and
  Beyond Me: Living a You-First Life in a Me-First World

I can say with all honesty that Pastor Paul Marshall's book, *Barefoot Revolution*, is one of only a handful of works that have actually helped me to go deeper with Jesus. It's practical, personal, and challenging. Most of all, it's the passionate cry from the heart of an author who wants Christ-followers to experience the embrace of God's love in a more intimate way—and then to share that with a hurting, broken world. This book will constantly nudge you to leave behind "life as is" for a radical ˜ ˜ ˜   all of your heart.
  –John David Kudrick, editor, writer, ar

Paul tackles the perennial issue of Christianity without substance, and harnesses Christian thinkers historical and recent to call us to a hope and a future. He illustrates the enlivening principles of a life based on spiritual knowledge with many stories of such lives lived on his watch, reinforced with practical steps for implementation both in personal and church life. This book will not just inform you—it will inspire you to live, borrowing from Parker Palmer, "the life that wants to live in me."

   –Costa Mitchell, National Director of The Association of Vineyard Churches of South Africa and author of *Giving Leadership: Taking Others with You on a Journey to Destiny*

Barefoot Revolution has important things to say about the fundamental challenges of Christian living, rising above the ordinary, and never accepting the inadequate. It is both encouraging and challenging. The writing style abounds in colorful and arresting phrases that make you stop in your tracks and think. There are frequent stimulating and thought-provoking questions both for personal challenge and group discussion, and many an opportunity to stop and meditate on the glories of the grace of God.

   –Dr. Barry Chant, author and teacher, co-founder and founding principal of Tabor College, Australia, and author of *Living in the Image of God*

Barefoot Revolution is a very balanced look at the reality that a focused Christian life simply doesn't "just happen." This book would be a real blessing to anyone who wants to get serious about following Jesus, and who is hungry for more.

   –Thora Anderson, Associate Pastor, Vineyard North Phoenix

Paul Marshall's book, *Barefoot Revolution*, speaks to a gaping black hole in Western, contemporary Christianity. It shows the way to a radical rediscovery of both the inward and outward life of a true disciple of Jesus.

   –Rob Norman, Senior Pastor, Southland Church, Adelaide, Australia

Undergirded with life-giving theology and illustrated by practical experience, *Barefoot Revolution* sends a fresh and insightful call to dare to follow Jesus truly from the heart.

   –Rick Williams, church planter, teacher, and coach

Paul Marshall's new book, *Barefoot Revolution,* offers an important and rare blend of orthodoxy in discipleship and intimate and transformational fellowship with Christ—it will simplify and revolutionize your walk with Christ.

   –Rev. Thom Gardner, President, Restored Life Ministries, Inc., and author of *Healing the Wounded Heart: Removing Obstacles to Intimacy with God*

Barefoot Revolution touches a nerve. With prophetic edge, Paul Marshall takes us beyond what is and shows us what should and can be.

–David Macmillan, former missionary with WEC International, Bible teacher, and leader of *Wingspan* Prayer Equipping Ministry (www.wingspanprayer.org)

BAREFOOT
REVOLUTION

Biblical Spirituality for Finding God

PAUL MARSHALL

PARACLETE PRESS
BREWSTER, MASSACHUSETTS

2018 First printing

Barefoot Revolution: Biblical Spirituality for Finding God

Copyright © 2018 by Paul Marshall

ISBN 978-1-61261-959-0

Library of Congress Cataloging-in-Publication Data
Names: Marshall, Paul A., 1948- author.
Title: Barefoot revolution : biblical spirituality for finding God / Paul Marshall.
Description: Brewster, Massachusetts : Paraclete Press Inc., 2017. | Includes bibliographical references.
Identifiers: LCCN 2017049552 | ISBN 9781612619590 (trade paper)
Subjects: LCSH: Spirituality—Christianity. | Spiritual life—Christianity.
Classification: LCC BV4501.3 .M27525 2017 | DDC 248.4—dc23
LC record available at https://lccn.loc.gov/2017049552

10 9 8 7 6 5 4 3 2 1

Published by Paraclete Press
Brewster, Massachusetts
www.paracletepress.com

Printed in the United States of America

Contents

*To Bec: the most beautiful, pure-hearted person I know,
love of my life—you lift me higher.*

*To Eliza, Reuben, Meg, Alice and Judah:
I pray you discover God's love
and thrive in the footprints of Jesus—
I am proud of you and
I love you no matter what.*

*To mum and dad:
you have blessed me by your faith and generous love
in sunshine and shadows—I love you.*

PART ONE

The Importance of a Spiritual Life

INTRODUCTION

Many Christians today experience the boredom and listlessness of spiritual exile, embracing the faith but feeling God is far away. If you feel that too, let me reassure you, you can find God again. This book will lead you on a transforming journey into God's loving and powerful presence, so don't give up on life-giving intimacy with him.

Your journey may be more positive, and having tasted something of God's presence, you are now wondering how you can live consistently in the flow of his life and kingdom. How can you find the sort of spiritual depth, power, and fruitfulness you see in the Bible or witness in others? How can the presence of God be so real that it shapes and gives wings to your daily life?

Whether we are distant or hungry for more, God wants us to grow—to become more like Jesus by moving on from where we are now. He loves us too much to leave us there. And as with any journey, we can only move forward from where we are right now. Where are you?

In God's grace, things are clear even if we aren't yet where we want to be. But spiritual exile is all muddle. If you are there, in such a muddle, you might believe God loves you, but not *experience* his love to displace your fear and guilt, heal your wounds, empower your life, or bless you with passion for life. God is effectively silenced and dethroned from our lives when we are in spiritual exile. His song in us ceases, hope withers, and our hearts are broken. We maintain appearances but live in a spiritual "flatland"—a dull, lifeless spiritual place devoid of loving intimacy with our Father.

We might engage in Christian activities but we are not conscious of the *presence* of God. The God-stories we tell mostly belong to someone else, reinforcing the sense that God only visits and works through others. Life's not all bad but we are inwardly dry and quietly desperate. Like the exiles by the rivers in Babylon, we sing songs to God but, if we are honest, our songs are an empty echo from an empty heart (see Ps. 137:1).

Do You Have a "Spiritual Life"?

Now before we resign ourselves to squashed hopes and unsatisfied hunger, we should ask an important question: *Do we actually have a "spiritual life"?*

I don't mean spiritual activities such as prayer or Bible study. Are we developing a dynamic, transforming relationship with God that brings him pleasure and enlivens our soul? The spiritual life refers to the ways by which the Holy Spirit's presence and work become real to us. It's the difference between theological ideas and an arresting experience of God—"a sense of Someone there" or the real presence of God.[1]

Extraordinary encounters like Paul's Damascus Road experience can happen, but most of the time our lives with God have genuine energy only when we are on a spiritual journey toward him. We must progress from our sin-limited consciousness about things toward Christ's higher one. This progression is not automatic for Christians and is much more contemplative than we might imagine. For many of us, the spiritual journey had a good start, but then stalled somewhere in "adolescence." Whether we lack a spiritual life or it has stalled before hitting its stride, we shouldn't be surprised to end up in a flatland.

If asked the way to life with God, Jesus would answer "follow me" every time. But this doesn't come naturally because love isn't natural to us in the way it is to God. *The inward discovery of God's love creates in us the readiness to willingly do what pleases him—something always characterized by love.* Experiencing and participating in God's love is integral to the spiritual life and explains why we end up spiritually flat when our spiritual life is thin.

Could it be that for lack of understanding or to sidestep the challenges of following Jesus, we just haven't given Christianity a proper test drive? And that because of this, we are perpetually deprived of the spiritual alertness that grace brings? As the English writer G. K. Chesterton wrote: "The Christian ideal has not been tried and found wanting. It has been found difficult and left untried."

If this is true, the way forward from a spiritual flatland is not to find a Christianity that is more appealing or relevant, or a church system that "works" more effectively. No. *Instead, we must engage in the humble task of truly learning how to live with God by developing skills for a real and consistent relationship with him.* And, I assure you, this is possible for every believer. Spiritual practices can train our souls to engage consistently at a heart level with God and respond positively to what he says.

In what ways does the spiritual part of your life facilitate a true spiritual journey toward God, and in what ways could it be more effective?

In these first couple of chapters, we will tackle some beautifully rich and powerful, but often not straightforward, aspects of the spiritual life: venturing into mysteries of the human heart, knowing spiritually, the issue of grace versus law, and the place of love in life with God and becoming one with him (this idea alone is enough to challenge most of us). The temptation is to deal lightly here, but for me these difficult areas are important and foundational, and I want to give everyone a shot at some grasp of them.

CHAPTER 1

Barefoot Revolution

Keep vigilant watch over your heart;
that's where life starts.

—PROVERBS 4:23 (MSG)

The spiritual life has a necessary outward expression, but its engine room is *inward*, where hunger for God germinates. As Jack Hayford writes, "God welcomes those into his presence who want him. The quest may be one of desperation or delight, of frantic need or a loving hunger for fellowship, but the motivation is clear—and so is his pleasure with it."[2]

The grace freeing us to step into the mystery of God's deeper way of being and doing (which Jesus called God's kingdom) originates with even just a mustard seed of insight into God or his love—in some way, we "see" it *inwardly*. This touches us deeply enough to rattle the cage of our will and, therefore, to respond with expressions of love for God. The significance of this inner work zooms into focus when we embrace the biblical fact: while our identity in Christ is as dearly loved children of God and saints, sinning comes naturally to us because of the Fall.[3] The very bent of our being, our will, deviates from God's will and, until grace reforms it, will draw us away from the presence of our Father.

Life with God, then, demands understanding in the heart, where we know things spiritually, where love and truth register, desire is forged, choices are made, and freedom is found. However this happens—by pure mercy or with the assistance of suffering, for example, human consciousness *must* be transformed.

In *Knowing Christ Today*, Dallas Willard made an important distinction between knowledge, belief, commitment, and profession. To know something involves the truth and accuracy of representation. For example, because of what automobile mechanics and brain surgeons *know,* they don't operate by guesswork but can consistently act in a certain way to effectively address a problem with a motor vehicle or a person's brain. When we *believe* something, we are ready to act on it, but we can believe what is false. *Commitment* is simply choosing to do something, whether or not there is belief or knowledge. And we can *profess* things without a shred of commitment. But faith, Willard concluded, is commitment to action based on spiritual knowledge and not a leap in the dark.

Devoid of spiritual knowledge, we have a greater propensity to shirk God's invitation to experience the deeper dimensions of reality experienced in his kingdom and presence. We are like the Beloved in Solomon's poem, cowering away from God because insight has not yet obliterated the lies telling us our voice is not sweet and our face not lovely (Song 2:14). Or we are like the character in a play who, unaware of the larger plot in the story, responds to situations in self-limiting ways. The audience groans, but, of course, the scriptwriter has given them the advantage of some natural insight.

The mystical aspect of the spiritual life shouldn't dissuade us from pursuing God because God is spirit and, like true happiness, enlightenment is always an inside job. Jesus taught that "the things that come out of a person's mouth come from the heart" (Matt. 15:18). His point: we live our lives from the inside out—from the heart. *The inner world of the spiritual shapes the outer world of activity.* The Bible, of course, embodies an Eastern worldview and effortlessly embraces this sort of rich spirituality. In the West—either because we don't understand it or lump all Eastern mysticism into the non-Christian "bad" basket—spirituality is mostly squeezed out and faith reduced to acquiring biblical information and declaring our belief in certain statements about God.

Is your current life of faith built upon an inward journey or just on outward activities?

Can We Know Things Spiritually?

Dallas Willard believed followers of Jesus today—along with everyone else—are in danger of rating knowledge in terms of mathematics and the sciences, and of concluding the central teachings of the Christian religion are mere belief or commitment. If we think knowing spiritually is pie-in-the-sky, we won't even try, and our spiritual life will atrophy. From the beginning, Christianity transformed the world because its core teachings were presented and accepted as knowledge about what is real and right.[4]

Spiritual knowledge didn't disappear because it doesn't exist anymore. Rather, human society in Europe squeezed it out in favor of modern knowledge represented by science. In fact, the historical causes of this "squeeze out" highlight the *instability* of the conclusion of modern Western society: that unlike our biblical heroes, you can't know things spiritually about God and about what is real and right.

Consider the Story of Moses

Moses bolted into the wilderness of the Sinai Peninsula forty years before the burning bush encounter catapulted him into God's mission. He hid there as a fugitive after slaying an Egyptian. He married, raised two sons in the desert near Mount Sinai, watching his father-in-law's sheep. Egypt might as well have been in another universe when he came upon the bush that kept burning as if fueled by an oil well but didn't burn up. As he approached it curiously, God manifested himself to him, commanding him to remove his sandals. Moses humbly obeyed. Then God ordered him back to Egypt! Like a salmon swimming upstream against the current of his fears, Moses obeyed.

Moses responded this way because he had some knowledge or higher consciousness of God. God said to him, "Take off your sandals, for the place where you are standing is holy ground" (Ex. 3:5). He removed his sandals, a mark in ancient times of respect and submission when visiting a host. In the host's domain, a guest relinquished the right to define what and how things were done. *This sort of abandonment to the will of God does not come naturally but only with inside knowledge of him and his love.* Under the powers afforded my hosts, I have both feasted and fasted, enjoyed belly laughs and been bored, found freedom and felt handcuffed. There are hosts—and there are hosts!

Moses discerned the divine presence immediately and hid his face. *God* is his Host, and he is in God's domain. Taking off his sandals symbolized a heart posture or attitude of surrender and readiness for God's defining voice. Moses is clay for the Potter, his disposition thrusting him into his sacred destiny in the Creator's hands, like visitors yielding themselves to the plans of their host. The Host is allowed to be host. God is allowed to be God. Moses was "barefoot"[5]—available and ready for God.

This attitude is like gold because it underpins the pulsing core of a vital spiritual life with God—discerning God's voice and willingly doing what is appropriate in his presence. Moving beyond spiritual adolescence to this maturity doesn't come naturally, but God won't strong-arm us. Instead he graciously enlightens us, liberating us into "barefoot" territory as a primary requirement for ongoing relationship. This explains why an insecure, goat-herding fugitive walked defiantly back into Egypt to foment revolution for God against the most powerful leader of the time. It also lights a trail leading beyond the spiritual flatland and proposes a cogent strategy for the church to incite a God-inspired revolution in the twenty-first-century world.

God's Presence is Not a Place

The significance of being "barefoot" emerges when we ask, "What does it mean to live in God's presence?" Of course, God is already present with us—everywhere. But Moses realized that God was present because God spoke to *him*, and the condition of his heart allowed him to hear God. We experience being with God when we can relate to him appropriately by discerning his voice and obeying it.

This is what Moses did consistently in the tabernacle during Israel's desert pilgrimage, shaping what it meant that Israel's temple was God's dwelling place (Ex. 25:8). By the time the first permanent temple was built in Jerusalem by King Solomon around the middle of the tenth century BC Israel's temple symbolized the residence of God at the center of national life.

Think about a town hall in the middle of a country town. The people of the town set their watches by the town hall clock and regularly check the bulletin board for activities. In a similar way, Israel was to calibrate life to the rhythm of God's heart, to make him the reference point, priority, and passion—the "center." All of the elements of life—marriage, children, work, relationships, possessions, time, and plans—were to be the subject of an ongoing conversation with God. *As they included and were present with God by hearing his word and obeying it, they were in his presence, and this is the nucleus of Christian spirituality.* We can be confident a Moses-like readiness for God is integral to finding God. Jesus taught, "seek and you will find" (Matt. 7:7).

Solomon's temple was destroyed in 586 BC when Babylon plundered and destroyed Jerusalem. Ezekiel had prophesied this from exile in Babylon. Despite being far from the temple itself, he also experienced God in Babylon as a glorious living being (see Ezek. 1:4–28).This helped him realize that living in God's presence is not about a place, but about how we relate to God. By the rivers of Babylon, Israel lamented its separation from God's presence, but Ezekiel called the people to fulfill *in their hearts* what the physical temple symbolized, and to include God in the equation of their everyday lives. This was the way out of their spiritual flatland even in the midst of physical exile! A 1970s pop classic, "Rivers of Babylon," borrowed from Psalms 137 and 19, capturing Ezekiel's gist:

> By the rivers of Babylon we sat and wept when we remembered Zion . . . for there our captors asked us for songs . . . How can we sing the songs of the LORD while in a foreign land? (Ps. 137:1–4)

> May these words of my mouth and this meditation of my heart be pleasing in your sight, LORD, my Rock and my Redeemer. (Ps. 19:14)

Back at the burning bush, relating to God for Moses meant being "barefoot"—stripped of delusions about his self-sufficiency and being ready to let God speak into all of life. We must do the same. Oswald Chambers said, ". . . everything that surrounds the ready soul is ablaze with the presence of God."[6] *The moment our inclination or inner choice makes us ready for God, he is there!* This is true of corporate worship times or sitting alone on the porch. He is always there, but now he is there *to you.* Your heart is home—at rest, secure, accepted, and soothed by healing words of love; free, called to change and be more alive. Appreciation for this sort of daily encounter with God seems to have been lost amidst the flatland of our spiritual lives. Instead, we might be seeking a miracle, like surfers after the perfect wave, but this is not enough for a vital spiritual life.

Historically, Israel refused to be ready for intimacy with God, and the result was spiritual exile. An impoverished spiritual life will rob believers of a hunger for God and lob them smack dab in the middle of a spiritual flatland, removed from his presence.

A Dangerous Assumption

If God manifested himself stunningly in burning-bush fashion, would we discern him speaking or call the fire department? Would we obey? Do we discern God speaking to *us* through our Bibles and then do what it says? These are not givens at all—they *don't* come naturally, even to God's loved children, because of our struggle against sin.

To hear or see in the full biblical sense means more than receiving an audible or visual message. It requires us to understand or gain insight with our *hearts*. Christian theology embraces the idea of prevenient grace, that is, any advances we make toward God are possible only because God has first made loving, desire-sparking advances toward us *that we can discern.*

When my wife, Rebecca, or I call out the name of our daughter Eliza across her school playground, she runs to hug us with delight. Others could call her name without this response, but our voices connect with something she knows in her heart. In other words, she perceives with her heart. On the other hand, if it isn't in Eliza's heart to do something we ask, she might ignore us, not "hear" us.

A simple word study of the key verbs used in the Bible for "hearing" and "seeing" supports the importance of the heart in receiving revelation from God. The verbs for *hearing* (*shama* in Hebrew and *akouo* in Greek) can also mean: to gain knowledge, learn, understand, hear and approve, or hear and obey. So when Genesis 22:18 says that all nations will be blessed because Abraham obeyed God's voice, this means he *heard* in a way that caused him also to obey. Similarly, at the Transfiguration, when God exhorted Peter, James, and John to listen to Jesus (see Matt. 17:5), he meant for them to follow Jesus, not just to receive information audibly. This applies whether we are simply reading the Bible or discerning God's voice by more "charismatic" means.

In the same way, verbs used for *seeing* include the broader idea of discovery, revelation, or spiritual vision. For example, those who are spiritually dull or unresponsive look but don't "see"—they don't have insight or "get it" (see Acts 28:26). The multitudes following Jesus heard his audible words, and many saw him perform miracles from front-row seats, but they didn't end up loving him or giving their allegiance to him because they didn't hear or see him in a full sense.

Maria's Story

Maria experienced the presence of God on a retreat when she was thirty. Up to then, prayer had been about requesting and looking for God's reply in external results—such as passing exams. Hungry for God, Maria found her spiritual life deepened. Her prayer life became about waiting, listening, seeing, feeling, and talking to God. She describes it as fluid and constant.

After having children, Maria and her youngest son walked into one of our Sunday services. She says, "We were the walking wounded, reeling from the ending of my thirty-year marriage." And the engine room of her recovery was that she had learned how to be aware of God's presence, allowing God to impress his healing love upon her fractured soul like sacred ointment.

Two years later, Maria was diagnosed with coeliac disease and bowel cancer. She says, "The first thing I saw after surgery to remove the cancer was Zephaniah 3:14–15, 17"—a call to rejoice because God has turned back your enemy and can save. By "saw" she meant that she hadn't just read but *experienced* the truth expressed in Zephaniah about God's desire and capacity to help his people, resulting in hope. As I write, nine years have passed since Maria was diagnosed with cancer. She is free of the disease and has a deep desire that others also experience the Person of Jesus and his healing presence.

"Soft Eyes"

Moses could discern God through a bush on fire and obey because his heart was made ready. He had what writer Parker Palmer calls "soft eyes," which are "open and receptive, able to take in the greatness of the world and the grace of great things," or sacred reality.[7] The Japanese self-defense art of *aikido* teaches the practice of "soft eyes" to rise above the defensive reflex of narrowing our eyes, which exacerbates the fight-or-flight response when we are threatened or surprised. Palmer uses this image to describe those who are able, when challenged by something new or beyond them, to widen their field of vision to take in more of the world rather than narrow their eyes in fear and cling to an old idea or a safe, self-preserving reality. With eyes wide open in wonder and belief, we can respond more positively by thinking a new thought or embracing a new truth rather than reacting in fear.

The flight from Egypt and forty years in the wilderness stretched Moses and formed him spiritually through the influence of Jethro, his wise and godly father-in-law.[8] This preparation for communion with God gave him "soft eyes." He still had weaknesses, but his discovery of God primed him for a greater level of obedience to God's will.

It's only when God's nature is formed in us that we don't question him when he speaks. We understand what God means when he speaks; what he says matters to us. Otherwise, we have no ear for anything but ourselves and what we want. Selfish people, for example, are deaf to the call to help others because the call doesn't connect with very much in their hearts—it's of a different nature. Love is a heart response from that part of us in which God's nature has taken shape. Knowing God's love frees us to love. Do you run lightly and freely into what pleases God, or does it feel more like trudging uphill while pushing a wheelbarrow?

In the mysterious grace of the spiritual life, we let God love us, and as the Holy Spirit reconfigures our hearts, the call to love becomes meaningful and life-giving. This was the story of Moses, and when a critical mass of Jesus-followers emulates him, the result is "a barefoot revolution."

How many of us are struggling to find a revolutionary edge because we have lived a superficial spiritual life?

Recovering the Use of Our Hearts

If readiness for God—that is, a willingness to hear and respond to God—requires a vibrant spiritual life, we face a problem today: *as materialism has grabbed the Western world by the throat over the past decades, we have neglected our souls and lost the ancient art of listening for God's voice.* Soul and spirit have been jettisoned in a hunt for happiness through shallow physical satisfactions. Until wealthy and successful idols of the materialism project became unhappy with their prosperity, we struggled to link our pain with our inner world. In this scenario:

> We might be forgiven for thinking that after all man is not made of soul and body, but of animal and machinery; that he does not need love, or beauty, or poetry, or art, or peace of mind; certainly he does not need to adore. All that he needs is material bread, sexual intercourse, oiling from time to time, and a tightening up of the screws that are so conspicuously loose.[9]

To follow Jesus into the deep, divine rhythms of God's kingdom, we need help in the broad areas of theology, training, and heart. *Theology* highlights the value of our intellect in the spiritual journey, helping us into the scope of heavenly thinking. Jesus theologized with Nicodemus, the Jewish religious leader, to introduce the idea of being spiritually "born again" into his mental framework (see John 3:1–21). Otherwise, Nicodemus would have languished on the sidelines of the kingdom due to ignorance about the need to pursue inward regeneration by the Holy Spirit. If, in our thinking, we attribute importance to performing in order to be loved, we'll try to do it and probably miss the mark altogether. If we don't understand that following Jesus involves sacrifice, we won't get very far before following him feels like a river too wide.

Smart, intellectual insight into Scripture, however, is never as powerful as even unvarnished truth creeping subversively into our souls. This is because studying the Bible per se will never save us. Study can be transforming, but only as it provides opportunity for the Spirit to reveal the thoughts or mind of Christ to us (see 1 Cor. 1:6–16).

Training equips us with skills for a spiritual life and for joining God in his work in the world. For example, we might believe God speaks through the Bible, but barely extract a few measly drops of living water because we don't know how to meditate. In the same way, without training, it's no surprise if we lack the confidence to pray for others or to witness to our neighbors.

Heart is about desire, hunger, a "barefoot" attitude. Do we have the inner conviction to apply our thinking or theology to our everyday life? Are we hungry enough to pursue God, to sharpen our skill set for a deeper spiritual life, or to fight to recover the use of a listening heart to hear God?

A Case for Mysticism

Properly used, the word "mystical" simply means the inward exercise of our souls toward God's love and the resulting outward expression of that love. True religion is always mystical because it gives us some conscious experience of union with God. For the saints and mystics,[10] Christian faith is a quest for the soul to be changed and made fit for intimate communion or oneness with God. Their goal: *to be one in heart and mind with God.* Jesus alluded to this quest when he prayed for us to be "in" the Father and the Son (see John 17:21).

Mysticism is essential because we must love God with our entire being, but this can't be achieved simply by knowing doctrines about God or imitating Christian practices. These things only symbolize spiritual experience. Unless we personally receive revelation by the Holy Spirit, we don't know what our doctrines and practices mean, so they can't lead us into what is real about God. They are no more transforming than meaningless repetitions from the unintelligent memory of a parrot. Reflect for example, on whether the Cross is merely a doctrine for you, or does it impact you with the liberating force of Spirit-revealed truth? For Christianity to meet the spiritual needs of our time, it will have to recover the fullness of biblical spirituality and exist in a form that is interior, spiritual, and mystical.

The Protestant merchant class that developed after the Industrial Revolution learned, in the hustle of business, to trust no one and get everything on paper—including their religion. They stopped embracing mystery and depending on the unseen action of God, as was necessary for an agrarian society depending on the seasons for crops. The Bible, rather than God, became the center of Protestant worship. Calvin's doctrines of predestination and irresistible grace appealed as ways of making their salvation a foregone conclusion. Instead of certainty, however, the Calvinist work ethic quickly developed to prove their salvation just in case their doctrines on paper weren't true!

Western evangelicals have elevated "purpose" beyond its good but lower-order station. In the *Westminster Catechism*, the chief end of man is to glorify God and to enjoy him forever. We proudly interpret this as our being of use to God, and we struggle with the "enjoy God" part. What we do for God can become serious business, not because we have discovered God's love, but because this is all that remains in the absence of mystical experience of it. But once we experience union with God (finding meaning and his love), we are freed from purpose to *playfulness*, expressed as sharing in the joy and beauty of God.

We serve God's purpose, but our service is "play" rather than a strict regimen qualifying us for his approval. It is entering God's story, not slavishly adhering to propositions about it. And the difference involves higher levels of consciousness that take us beyond the spiritual flatland. We are freed from fearful or prideful religious scheming and "have to" activities, to dally each day in spontaneous response to God's will for the moment. We are like the birds of the air and the lilies of the field, without worry and unsanctified responsibility for our future (see Matt. 6:25–34). Feeding the poor, worshiping God, and loving one another become joyful and beautiful in a way that refreshes and vitalizes our soul. This is because we "get to" share in the joy of God and his power to love, heal, restore, and create. Jesus calls his followers to this joy (John 15:9–11), and to the revolutionary force of such "playfulness," both to enliven our souls and to bless the world with restoration.

Does purpose or play best describe your life of faith? What does this mean for your on-going journey toward God?

The Coming of the Kingdom

Some Jews wanted the Messiah to be a military leader like King David, leading them to crush the Romans. Instead, Jesus ravished the hearts of hurt and guilty people with God's goodness as Isaiah had seen it seven hundred years earlier (see Isa. 61 and 42:1–4). The ministry and Cross of Christ was a cosmic assault of justice, mercy, love, and grace on the earth by the power of the Spirit—a messianic type of Jubilee year recalibrating back to the way it was before the human soul was plundered by sinful interactions. God was restoring his world for his glory.

This was no isolated campaign of blessing but part of the trajectory of God's cosmic story. The life we see in Eden, inspired by God for humans to live fully as his children and for his glory, had been spoiled by sin. Weeping over the ravages of slavery, broken relationships, betrayal, lust, and pride, he was acting in Christ to restore life as he had created it. The Lion of Judah roared mightily with expressions of love in the face of evil: sins were forgiven; people found their true identity as loved children of God; poor, sick, and brokenhearted people were restored; those suffering condemnation found acceptance; crying turned to joyful dancing. Blind Bartimaeus stepped into its healing light when he cried out to Jesus as he left Jericho for Jerusalem to face the Cross: "Son of David, have mercy on me!" (Mk. 10:47). Full of compassion and power, Jesus healed him. And then the Cross—a sublime expression of powerful mercy and love dealing with sin and death—sent ripples through the cosmos.

This tsunami of mercy is not an obscure idea, but a central theme in Old Testament prophecy concerning the last days.[11] Around 600 BC, Ezekiel prophesied a miraculous river of mercy flowing from underneath the temple and restoring the creation (see Ezek. 47:1–12). Its miraculous waters turned the Dead Sea's stagnant, salty wastewater fresh, and swarms of living creatures appeared. The banks of the river nurtured never-failing fruit trees, and their leaves provided healing. Like an animator adding color and movement to a lifeless scene, the waters from the temple transformed the desert into a perpetual oasis that was fruitful and teeming with life. The Creator was unleashing the full orb of his life-force, his very Spirit, to bless the world by restoring it.

Daniel had a vision of the Christ subverting the doomed value systems, cultures, and kingdoms of this world (see Dan. 2:44–45). With Christ's resurrection, God would inaugurate a new age in which God's kingdom of truth, healing, restoration, and grace would break into our "now." Restoration is part of the story until Jesus returns—when "the old order of things has passed away" and there is no more death, crying, and pain (see Rev. 21:4) because "the kingdom of the world has become the kingdom of our Lord and of his Messiah" (Rev. 11:15).

When God called Abram he promised to *bless* him or to bring him happiness and wellbeing, and to *bless* all peoples on earth through him (see Gen. 12:1–3). In the same way, we receive blessing from God, and as a worshipful response, we are called to partner with the Holy Spirit to bless our world. *We* are drawn into this end times Jubilee through a vital spiritual life, rendering us barefoot before God—with souls alive and ready to hear and obey, kneeling down, ready to receive blessing and to bless our world.

When Jesus quoted Isaiah 61 in the synagogue in Nazareth with the understanding his ministry would fulfill this prophecy he also said, "Today this scripture is fulfilled in your hearing" (Lk. 4:18–21). The kingdom had come but not fully as yet, so it makes sense that Jesus was saying the prophecy would be fulfilled throughout the time of the church on earth—through our lives.[12] On the day of Pentecost after the ascension of Jesus, the Holy Spirit came to empower his followers, writing another chapter of the same story of blessing (see Acts 2:16–21). As active participants in chapters yet to be written, our lives are meant to be anything but spiritually flat!

Something Must Shift Inside Us

Now let me save you some hard yards. Simply striving to be more "barefoot" or to claw our way beyond spiritual adolescence and flatness won't work. It's not a matter of willpower or self-motivation. Instead, something must shift inside us—self must be subverted to make way for the kingdom. We must be able to proclaim our readiness for God like the psalmist: "I run in the path of your commands, for you have broadened my understanding" (Ps. 119:32). It won't fall like manna from the sky but requires, amidst the mechanics of soul and spirit, that God's Spirit plant within us the sacred seed of the knowledge of his love. We must return to a truly biblical spiritual life—to things that may defy rationality and challenge our ideas about what is important but are essential for true knowledge of God.

Because God is love, to say we want to find God's life is to say we want to find a life catalyzed and defined by *love*. This doesn't come easily to us in the receiving or the giving away, but both are essential.

For Discussion

1. Discuss the concept of a "spiritual flatland." In view of this, how would you describe your own life with God?

2. What is meant by "a spiritual life," and why do you think it is important for finding God? In what way is the journey toward God necessarily inward and mystical in nature?

3. Explain your view about whether we can *know* God or his love spiritually. What are the implications of your view for your own spiritual expectations and journey?

4. What does it mean to be "barefoot" as described in the story of Moses, and why is it important? How is this heart-attitude formed in us, and to what extent do you think it is formed in you?

5. Biblically, what does it mean to *hear* or *see*, and how effectively do you think you can do it? Explain.

6. Do you think it is true that we tend to neglect our souls and have lost the art of hearing God? Explain the balance of *theology*, *training*, and *heart* in your own spiritual life.

7. Describe God's cosmic story and the difference between *purpose* and *playfulness* for our active participation in what God is doing in the world. How does it become "play"?

CHAPTER 2

Resurrecting the Life of Love

He who follows the Lamb in His way comes at last
to where the Lamb Himself is.

—G. STEINBERGER[13]

With notable consistency, Jesus said, "follow me," to anyone seeking salvation and a better life. His gist: if we follow him "in his way," we will find ourselves where he himself is—beyond the flatland and close to God. The New Testament trumpets *love* as the heartbeat of Christ's way and the core characteristic of life with God from start to finish. This is because God *is* love. And for this reason, the Desert Fathers—early Christian monks known for their powerful wisdom teachings—insisted the spiritual life *is* love. A spiritual life without love as a central cog is adolescent; with love comes revelation, spiritual maturity, and revolution. The flatland is flat because, in that place, we struggle to receive God's love, to be made expectant or hopeful by it, or to genuinely express it to others in soul-liberating ways. In other words, we don't follow the Lamb "in his way" at all. We just think we do. As a committed Jesus-follower, I find this thought sobering. How do you find yourself responding to it?

Somehow, intuitively, we know love is of a higher order of things because, deep down, we want to be loved much more than we want to find the right answers to things. And when we are loved or can love, we touch the soul-enlivening pulse of it. Can you identify with this from your experience? Genuine love is to the soul what oxygen is to the body—the way our soul breathes. Self-depreciation and selfishness for example, leave our souls gasping to breathe. But genuine love doesn't come naturally to us because of the Fall; it must now be resurrected in us by the Holy Spirit, underscoring the importance of the spiritual life.

Higher Consciousness for Finding God

Jesus taught the supreme commandment was all-out love for God, and that in doing this we will naturally also fulfill a second commandment: to love others as well as we love ourselves (see Matt. 22:37–39). Nothing wishy-washy here: *if we desire to find God, we can't afford to indulge our natural inclination to focus on self.*

A Pharisee attempted to trap Jesus with a riddle about which written commandment was most important for life with God, and his answer is significant: life with God is not about fulfilling one commandment or another, but in fulfilling *all* the commandments by learning about love. The Pharisee's spiritual consciousness—or simply, his awareness of what God taught to be right and true (the Law)—could only muster a self-focused sort of passion for God. Jesus offered to ramp up his consciousness level by teaching that *deeper life with God hinges on developing the inward capacity for genuine love.* This makes good sense if God is love and if all his dealings with us are to bring us into oneness with himself as Jesus prayed (see John 17:21).

Now, God's love is not a guarantee of this oneness because the first commandment rejects universalism—the idea that all people will ultimately be saved regardless of their attitude toward God because "God is love." But Jesus *is* saying love is integral to life with God. This higher consciousness flipped the focus of religion on its head—from doing right to earn brownie points with God for *you*, to an inward attitude of true love and service to others. Elsewhere Jesus taught: if we serve others in need we actually serve *him* (see Matt. 25:31–46).

In Luke's Gospel, this encounter involves an expert in the law (see Lk. 10:25–37). He offers the correct answer by taking the most central prayer in Jewish worship—the *Shema*, based on Deuteronomy 6:4–5, which calls for wholehearted love for God—and adding the law of neighbor-love from Leviticus 19:18. Jesus affirms his answer and adds: "Do this and you will live." However, the lawyer then exploited the ambiguity surrounding the interpretation of the law by asking, "And who is my neighbor?" It is unlikely, in the first century, anyone except the people of Israel qualified as neighbors, but Jesus deployed the Parable of the Good Samaritan to challenge this small-hearted interpretation.

A man is violently robbed by bandits, stripped of his clothes, and left half-dead. It's impossible to classify him as Jew or Gentile, friend or enemy. He is simply a human being, a neighbor, in need. A priest and a Levite see the man but pass by on the other side of the road. With no evident religious excuse, they do nothing for the wounded man. In contrast, a despised Samaritan—not a holy man but merely a traveling merchant—sees the man, is moved by compassion, and goes above and beyond the call of duty to risk his life and spend his money to care for him.

Interestingly, priests and Levites had status, not because of their training or selection but because they were born into priestly families—*"their ancestry and association with the temple commended them as very pious people, not their performance."*[14] Today there is a tendency to think God rips up the scorecard and evaluates us merely on the basis of our ancestry—that we are Christians—rather than on our actual practice of his Word. But here, it is exactly the Samaritan's performance that distinguishes him from the two holy men in the eyes of Jesus. Performing to *qualify* for God's love screams against grace and is not life-giving, but performing from an *involvement* in God's heart of love, like this Samaritan did, is somehow integral to receiving eternal life. "Do this and you will live!" (Lk. 10:28b).

With this story as a reference point, how would Jesus assess your performance in reflecting God's heart of love?

Historically, the church has dumbed this down because of the challenges presented by the sort of spiritual life required to crank our hearts over to kick-start such a benevolent life. Ironically, it is too removed from the bottom line! But the saints and mystics made it their bottom line to fulfill the prayer of Jesus and enter into union with God via a natural participation in his mind and heart of love. Affectionate feelings for Christ on Sunday don't cut it as the sign of this oneness, but being and acting like him in the mundane of life on Mondays does.

Christians should be known for Good Samaritan-class, above-and-beyond love as they fill the earth with the knowledge of God (see Isa. 11:9) and trigger choruses of worship by making people glad in God's goodness (see Ps. 67:3–4). *The Christian response to the onslaught of secular ideologies and science-based "new atheism" isn't just to dogfight over philosophies, but to cultivate a vital spiritual life that generates authentic power and radical love.* Sadly, being a "Good Samaritan" has become generic in wider society for someone who does any sort of "good deeds," rather than distinguish Christ's followers for their brand of radical love.

If a friend enthusiastically expresses love to us, but her aims, actions, and perspectives on things clash with ours, we won't feel much oneness between us. The same is true with God. As Hannah Whitall Smith wrote:

> To be one with Christ is too wonderful and solemn and mighty an experience to be reached by any overflow or exaltation of mere feeling. He was holy, and those who are one with Him will be holy also.[15]

This echoes Paul's teaching that when the Holy Spirit controls our lives (which speaks about the spiritual life), he will produce the fruit of love, kindness, and goodness in us (see Gal. 5:22–23).

Soul Wealth

You might be thinking, "Wow, that's beyond me!" and you're right, of course (it is God's undertaking). But before you dodge what is vital for life with God, let me invite you into some beautiful grace: *God gives us the soul resources for a life of love by loving us first.*

The dilemma facing humanity is we have a cavernous need to be loved and accepted but can't ever be good enough to be worthy of it. We contort our lives trying to escape our painful or ordinary "now" for some other time when we will be pain-free or successful. We try to be someone we are not who is more "acceptable" according to the rules of society and (sadly) religion[16] by hiding or trying to remove the not-so-good in us. *But God solves the dilemma with a divine choice of love that swallows up all of its heavyweight complexity in something stunningly simple and deeply sacred: he decides to love us despite the not-so-good in us![17]* Franciscan priest and spiritual director Richard Rohr well makes the point that God will call us to outgrow whatever is counter to our well-being for his glory, but our worthiness is, yes, a gift! We must simply recognize the truth about ourselves and receive God's grace in Christ. We are left to bask in our identity as God's loved children, his people, and in his unwavering delight in us. *This* is what makes us fall in love with God—to want to contemplate him—and frees us to bless our world.

Consider your identity in Christ. Are you a loved child of God, or do you struggle to accept that you are worthy?

Another by-product of letting God love us is that he gifts us with the peace of Christ. This inner peace powerfully scatters fear, sends self-absorption hiking, births dreams, stretches horizons, and makes heavy souls free and light because:

It is the presence and promise of Jesus to be with me. Inner peace never stands alone; it is always experienced in divine relationship . . . it is not the lack of noise or a mood, but it is a relational grace, guarding my heart.[18]

When our cry for acceptance is answered, this soul-security and wealth inclines us to be rich toward God and others. For example, a sinful woman expressed extravagant love by decanting a jar of expensive perfume on Christ's feet because she had been forgiven much (Lk. 7:36–50). Jesus humbly washed his disciples' feet because he knew that his authority and destiny were secure (John 13:3). Thomas à Kempis, a German monk and writer in the 1400s, captured the idea when he prayed, "Let love possess me so that I rise up above myself. . . ."[19]

To experience good things at God's hand is one thing, but to be *aware* of his love and made rich by it is a thoroughly inward and spiritual exercise. As Paul makes clear in Romans 5:5, *the Holy Spirit* fills our heart with God's love. This explains why Jesus healed ten lepers but only one came back, and why most people living in the prosperous West have only a scrap of love for God.

In James Cameron's blockbuster movie *Avatar*, the Na'vi, a race of extraterrestrial humanoids who inhabit the jungle moon of Pandora, greet each other by saying: "I see you." This greeting, practiced in some African countries, is more than just recognizing the physical presence of the other person. It is recognition of their inward substance. One freezing winter morning while waiting at a railway station, the warm rays of the sun found me, and my heart found its voice: "I see you, Lord." I was "seeing" God's soul or who he is—the beauty of his goodness and love—and this "seeing" made me wealthy within myself, and rich toward him and toward others (see Ps. 27:4–6).

The baptism of Jesus is a profound example of this beautiful grace: "He received honor and glory from God the Father. The voice from the majestic glory of God said to him, 'This is my dearly loved Son, who brings me great joy'" (2 Peter 1:17 NLT). *It heals and energizes our soul when someone believes in us like this even when our performance is shoddy.* When we notice God is looking at us and delighting in his own workmanship, acceptance and hope flood in to make us soul-millionaires. "If I am left to myself, behold, I become nothing but mere weakness, but if You for an instant look upon me, I am instantly made strong and filled with new joy" (Kempis).[20]

Barriers to Letting God Love Us

We often find it difficult to let God love us because this would mean we are needy of love or grace. We would have to admit we have done something wrong, couldn't make it on our own, failed, didn't know the answer, or weren't the best. Western culture teaches us to despise these traits, so in fear we cover up the truth, and work to prove ourselves. Inwardly we scream out for the ointment of love and grace to obliterate our shame, guilt, and fear but opt for earning adulation rather than allowing God's loving kindness to penetrate our protective barriers. Can you think specifically about how you behave in this way?

Many people I meet won't speak up in a group for fear that what they say will reflect badly on them. Our worth can be attached to having the right answer or saying things that impress people. For the same reason, I found myself deliberately covering over the fact that I didn't know what to do when I started a new job. I could have asked for help, and it may have reflected badly on me. But I wouldn't be cowering or buying the lie that if you don't know the answer, express a different viewpoint, or even say something poorly or something that is downright *wrong*, this has anything to do with your identity or worth as a person.

Self-condemnation, self-preservation, and self-promotion gobble up a lot of room in our hearts, leaving little space for receiving or expressing love. God's love enters our experience when we stop covering up, proving, and earning, and instead own up to the fact we feel like crying, we are in pain, we don't have answers, our dreams have gone pear-shaped, we are afraid or ashamed, we have sinned, or prayer is drudgery for us. God snaps up these honesty-moments to detonate his powerful mercy inside us and transform the impoverished regions of our soul.

Our experience of God's love can also be limited if we cannot discern the flood of God's love that has already happened. I think of the overarching, unprecedented gifts of God's love in Christ, such as his choice for us in eternity past that gives us an unshakeable identity as his "loved ones," forgiveness of sins, adoption as his children, the giving of the Holy Spirit, and our resurrection from the dead to live on as eternal souls. So how is it possible we could miss this flood?

Individualism has fixated us on what is happening for *me* in the present moment. Our understanding of God's love then becomes about our experience of God *now* and less focused on the overarching, already-expressed evidences of his love. They are inadvertently downgraded from gifts of love (which delight the soul), to doctrinal rights or "givens" for us as believers (which barely impact our emotions). We might champion the doctrine behind these overarching gifts and honor Christ for them, but be unable to embrace their fulfillment in our lives. God's love in Christ *is* a flood, but by understanding God's love only in terms of *me* and *now*, we can miss the flood that has already happened for all of us!

Of course we should pray, "Let your kingdom come now," but God's love will seem fickle, inconsistent, and hard to find if we miss the flood and depend solely on what God does for us *now* to experience his love. What if God doesn't do what we want? Besides, the overarching, already-expressed evidences of God's love are the basis for our expectation in faith for his ongoing love. What weight do you place on the flood of God's already-expressed evidence of his love versus your experience of God *now*? Reflect on how this might impact your spiritual life.

Learning from the Dead Sea

Now let's assume we have allowed God to love us, and we feel inwardly wealthy. Is this enough to sustain a life with God? Not according to Jesus! He pointed to the *outgoing* nature of the Spirit-filled life—that receiving the Holy Spirit meant not only being deeply satisfied by an inner spring of living water filling us to the brim, but also being a conduit of living water to others from the overflow (see John 7:37–39). The Dead Sea is lifeless because it receives water from the Jordan River but gives none away. Whatever it receives becomes too stagnant and salty to support life, highlighting a foundational spiritual principle: *a vital spiritual life will have both an inflow and an outflow.*

If you drew up two columns, placing instances of *inflows* of God's love into your life in one column and *outflows* in the other, what would it tell you?

Not surprisingly, then, Jesus sent out the Twelve with the words *freely you have received, freely give* (Matt. 10:8b). He taught that both asking for forgiveness and forgiving others was distinctive of his followers (see Lk. 11:4a). And among the final words he spoke to his disciples before his execution, Jesus said:

> The Father has loved me by championing my well-being, and now I have loved you in the same way. If you stay mindful of my love for you and in this way also love others by being proactive for their good, your joy will be complete. This is how to find well-being for your own soul (John 15:9–11, my paraphrase).

The Cross looms large, and Jesus reaches for what matters—sizzling spiritual insight upon which the fulfillment of the disciples' leave-everything-to-follow aspirations will hinge. Flatland demons torment us with despair that our Jesus-aspirations are nonsense, but those taunts are not without some basis if we ignore the spiritual savvy of Jesus here: *you must both personally discover God-quality love and love others in the same way.* This exposes the understanding Jesus had of life with God as a sphere or an economy of genuine love with an inflow and an outflow. We live in it, or participate "in" God as we both receive love and give it away to others. This two-sided dynamic is reflected in a paradox, a puzzle serving as a spiritual on-ramp that pilgrims must first decipher before accessing the spiritual highway.

A Confusing Paradox: Making Sense of Things

On one hand, we can do *nothing* good or bad to make God love us more. God's love has nothing to do with our performance, because his love is intrinsic to the existing beauty and magnificence of himself; it is not something we can create but simply receive as a gift. God sent Jesus to die for us to establish our identity as loved children of God "while we were still sinners" (see Rom. 5:8). On the other hand, to please God or to participate in his life and kingdom requires we continue to do *something* in positive response to his love. Jesus taught that those who "hear the word of God and obey it" are blessed (see Lk. 11:27–28).

THE PARADOX GOVERNING LIFE WITH GOD

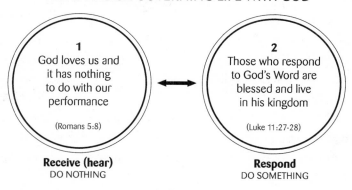

1
God loves us and it has nothing to do with our performance

(Romans 5:8)

2
Those who respond to God's Word are blessed and live in his kingdom

(Luke 11:27-28)

Receive (hear)
DO NOTHING

Respond
DO SOMETHING

FIGURE 1

Foundationally, our response includes wholehearted love and worship, but at some point that response must be about concrete actions that please and serve God—blessing our world to make people glad in the greatness of God (Ps. 67:3–4). As we respond our experience of God leads to further response and deeper experience of him. Without some synthesis between these two sides of the paradox, our life with God will soon run out of gas.

The Synthesis of the Sides

Contemplative people champion "being" before God while activists champion "doing." But real life in the presence of God is found in the synthesis of the two. This is the place of peace, rest, and transformation. Without spoiling the place of each, we must let them be part of the whole and work together like pedals on a bicycle. The apostle Paul unmistakably taught this synthesis. For example, in consecutive verses to the Ephesians he declared our salvation is a gift of grace, not a reward for works (see Eph. 2:8–9), *and* that God has planned good works for each of us to do (see Eph. 2:10)—no doubt to serve the coming of God's kingdom. Niels Bohr, the Danish physicist who won the Nobel Prize in Physics in 1922, noted, "The opposite of a fact is falsehood, but the opposite of one profound truth may very well be another profound truth." *For vital life with God, it is true that we must both do nothing and something.*

Let's unpack this a bit through the lens of the visit Jesus made to the home of Martha and Mary (see Lk. 10:38–42). Martha fussed around in the kitchen to be hospitable while Mary sat at his feet drinking in his words. Mary's hospitality—to make the words of Jesus welcome in her heart—hit the mark with Jesus, so he refused Martha's request to tell Mary to lend her a hand. Jesus seems to value intimacy over busy work for him, but we can be intimate without any commitment or dedication as much as we can do things for him without true devotion. To extrapolate this story to mean that we need not do anything for him seriously limits the dimensions of the relationship and misses the point. *It isn't about a contemplative life versus an active one, but the sort of hospitality to the Word that frees us to do what it says.*[21]

Part of our struggle is in recognizing the Christ who calls us to sit quietly like Mary to receive love and offer adoration as the very same Christ who is at the very same time waging battle through his Spirit-empowered people to love the marginalized, save the lost, and heal the sick. His tears of love and joy when we seek worshipful intimacy with him are difficult to distinguish from his sweat from the battle. It is "both-and," not "either-or." Like Mary, we should leave our distracting activities to sit at his feet, listen to him, and adore him (as our priority and an end in itself because God is ultimate), but does this mean *not* doing other things that express God's heart and therefore also give him pleasure? Wouldn't sitting at the feet of Jesus as objects of his love and truly hearing his words free us to want to do these other things?

The well-documented spiritual malaise of many churches today stems foundationally, I believe, from a failure to decipher the spiritual on-ramp—confusion about our paradox and the subsequent failure to find a real synthesis of its two sides. When we struggle to embrace God's no-cost love, legalism gets a foot in the door, threatening the synthesis by harmfully entrenching us in the second side under the heavy burden of performing for God's affectionate attention. If we can't get our head around the *nothing* part of our paradox (fueled by our need to be self-sufficient and in control), we ignore it and make it all about doing *something*. When a shortfall of love drives our response, it violates the synthesis I am referring to, but doing *something* freely on the wings of insight into God's love is not the same. Being pushed (or pushing ourselves) to perform for God is not good, but again this is starkly different from choosing to do what our Lord asks of his followers because we truly love him. As the apostle Paul wrote:

> For Christ's love compels us, because we are convinced that one
> died for all, and therefore all died. And he died for all, that

those who live should no longer live for themselves but for him who died for them and was raised again (2 Cor. 5:14–15).

Deciding to respond out of whatever we have now (see Phil. 2:1–5)—whether a little or a lot of insight into his love—is the way to receiving more.

A further threat to this synthesis is the temptation to think we should only do what tickles our fancy. This offers some protection against legalism, but it also risks the fullness of God's life because he is always calling us from what we want to what he wants (i.e., to come under divine authority that expresses God's love).[22] Unless our spirituality and morality enables this, what good is it?

A common tendency today is to slog at performing to earn God's love, but then to resist any call to obey him because it smacks of performance; we are deceived into working hard at the inverse of the paradox. The call to obedience is seen to lack grace, but as Dallas Willard wrote, "Grace is not opposed to effort, it is opposed to earning."[23] The real issue is our inability to stop performing for God's love and to *receive* grace. Letting God love us liberates us to serve him.

Jesus didn't prescribe a rest from doing things; he prescribed doing *different* things—*his* sort of things—if we want to live freely and lightly (see Matt. 11:28–30).

"Contemplatives in action" describes many of our heroes from the Bible and throughout church history, as people who did not neglect either side of our paradox or the synthesis of the two. They weren't clones, with some emphasizing one side in the synthesis, and some the other. But whatever the expression, they found real synthesis. Activists without love may have the answer, but they are no more a part of the answer than contemplatives who find God's love but do nothing. *Distortion on either side of the paradox scuttles the synthesis and consigns us to the flatland.*

The apostle Paul's letters reveal a deep, defining appreciation of God's grace, the "do nothing" part of the paradox, forged by his

Damascus Road experience. But, interestingly, his earthly life goal was framed in terms of "doing something" in response to it: "we make it our goal to please him, whether we are at home in the body or away from it" (2 Cor. 5:9). He understood his life vocation to be for the praise of God's glory (see Eph. 1:11–12). The *nothing* and the *something* didn't replace or diminish each other but worked together as the basis of Paul's God-life. Is it any different for you or me?

The life of Jesus embodied a synthesis of the paradox. His Father honored him *before* his ministry kicked off, and he could say, after crossing paths with the Samaritan woman at the well, "My food is to do the will of him who sent me and to finish his work" (John 4:32–34). He clearly meant loving this woman by being a conduit of salvation and restoration to her (see vv. 35–36). This is not legalism but "synthesis," and a deeper way of being with God. It steered Jesus to the awful cost of the Cross but it deeply nourished his soul. In the synthesis, he found his destiny and so do we.

Where do you see yourself in terms of a synthesis between the *nothing* and *something* sides of the paradox? Can you pinpoint specific personal struggles in moving toward synthesis?

The Life of Love or "Immersed Life"

Love energized and directed the life of Jesus. He transitioned constantly and seamlessly between the two sides of our paradox—receiving his Father's love and giving it away, and for this reason we can call it a *life* of love. To burrow into deeper spirituality, his Father, who is the embodiment of love, was flowing into him and out from him to bless the world. In this sense Jesus lived a life *immersed* in or deeply involved with his Father, and he calls us to *immerse* ourselves in, around, for, and with him.[24]

Late in life, the apostle John pulled back the covers on the profound mystical reality that love and God are synonymous:

Dear friends, let us love one another for love comes from God. Everyone who loves has been born of God and knows God. . . . God is love. Whoever lives in love, lives in God, and God in them (1 John 4:7, 16b).

In other words, when God's love softens us to invite his Spirit to take up residence in us and to have the run of the house (see John 3:3–5), love moves in and has the run of the house too. His life manifests itself as an economy or sphere of love, and we begin to live *in* that sphere—the circle of God's life and the circle of our lives start to overlap substance-wise. We participate "in" love that drives out our fear, rather than living in fear and over against love (as a theological concept). Rather than struggling in separation from God to find or express his love, we are being united with him and naturally encounter and express his DNA. *To experience genuine love or to express it is to experience the flow of God within us.* In this sense, love and God are like two sides of one coin: each side gives access to the other. This is the dynamic, the "furniture" of our life in God: God answers the deep longing in our soul with the ointment of his love; we adore him *and* decide to develop the tendency to cooperate proactively with the Holy Spirit to serve the well-being of others (which also gives God pleasure). *It is the flow of God's life through us, but we are not passive because it flows through our prayers, hands, possessions, gifts, and friendships with the needy.*

Many believers struggle to experience this sacred sphere despite having invited the Spirit to reside in them—often because we aren't ready for it. We haven't learned, by participating in good spiritual practices, to delight in heavenly things. Our hearts have not been made pure enough yet to be at peace with being who we truly are rather than striving for a false self who is more "successful" or "beautiful." To the Desert Fathers this peace or "rest" was important because it meant being free to be carried "Wherever Love itself, or the Divine Spirit, sees fit to go," as Thomas Merton once put it.[25]

Inviting the Spirit to reside in us is a good start, but we must also want to be truly united with Christ or immersed in him. And we must make practical decisions for the sort of life—marked for example, by times of solitude, repentance, worship, Christ's acts of love, and prayer—that will give the Spirit opportunity to gradually establish our true selves unshackled from the compulsions of the world, and bless us with this rest. For the Desert Fathers, it was from this place of peace and freedom the believer and Christ could become "one Spirit"; from here the human spirit secretly laid hold of the sphere of God's life and love.[26]

Out of sublime rest, Jesus lived and breathed this sacred sphere. The Father's lavish love caused inward sparks, creating an appetite for Father-time to exchange affection, find soul-energy, and shape a subversive vision for restoring Creation: "Jesus often withdrew to lonely places and prayed" (Lk. 5:16). Topped up with love and the vibe of the Father's heart, practical service was effortless: "And I will do whatever you ask in my name, so that the Father may be glorified in the Son" (John 14:13).

Because he lived in the sphere of love, it wasn't paradoxical even for the Messiah to serve others: "I, the Messiah, did not come to be served, but to serve, and to give my life as a ransom for many" (Matt. 20:28 TLB). His ultimate act of loving service was to lay down his life to save us: "Greater love has no one than this, to lay down one's life for one's friends" (John 15:13).

What's more, Jesus rallied his followers to reflect his life in the sphere of God's love: "A new command I give you: Love one another. As I have loved you, so you must love one another" (John 13:34). He made a powerful connection between the life of love and living in God's presence: "Anyone who loves me [has received my love] will obey my teaching. My Father will love them, and we will come to them to make our home with them" (John 14:23, my comment added).

How does this discussion enrich your idea of what it means to follow Jesus?

Love is integral to following the Lamb "in his way"—our ticket out of the flatland and into revolution.

Beyond Adolescent Spirituality

To neglect love is to saddle ourselves with an adolescent spirituality. This is not pigeonholed by its lack of passion or commitment to "spiritual" things, but by the absence of what matters to God. Because God is love, what matters to him will *always* express love. So when we receive love and learn to love, our spirituality "grows up." The reason it's a grown-up spirituality is it can position us closer to God: when we love, the circle of our lives overlaps with the circle of God's life. We are more one with him. Adolescent spirituality isn't all bad, but it tends to major on marginal things at the expense of core expressions of God's love. For this reason, it doesn't help our trek toward God very much.

Because even loved souls struggle with sin, we struggle to conceptualize much more than a limited version of genuine love. This means we must discover it if our spirituality is to grow up and we are to scurry from the spiritual flatland.

The Bible is brimming with insights to inform and fuel our discovery process, and some key biblical perspectives on genuine love are explained briefly below.

Genuine Love Results from a Higher Level of Spiritual Development

Genuine love is a fruit of the Spirit (see Gal. 5:22–23)—the Holy Spirit elevates us to higher levels of consciousness, meaning we see, think and act more like Jesus. *The Christian life is not about straining at doing right, but becoming different sorts of people for whom genuine love flows naturally.*

At the lowest level of consciousness, we serve ourselves and the demands of our ego for attention and significance because the love column in our soul-ledger is "in the red." We barely register the needs of others—what others? At the highest level of consciousness, however, sacrificing ourselves for the well-being of others, à la Jesus, would both be meaningful and boost our sense of well-being. This is in harmony with the New Testament teaching that love is the primary mark of spiritual maturity (see 1 Cor. 13:1–13 and Gal. 5:6), and that Christian spirituality is supposed to transform and lift us upward toward Christ in terms of our human development:

> And the Lord—who is the Spirit—makes us more and more like
> him as we are changed into his glorious image (2 Cor. 3:18b NLT).

The mystics pursued an interior journey of the soul, progressing through levels of spiritual development and culminating in a spiritual union with God or the life of love. More recently, the work of psychology shows the progressive stages of human development we should expect if we are growing spiritually.[27] Combining the two, in *Falling Upward*, Richard Rohr conceptualizes the first half of life as the necessary task of surviving successfully—making ourselves secure, chalking up some achievements, finding significance and a sense of our self. In the second half necessary suffering—failure, loss, or disappointment—helps us discover our limits and powerlessness, turn our soul toward God, and through epiphanies to discover God's love as a focus for our lives rather than our earthly security and achievements.

Where are you in Rohr's two journeys? Are you on a progressive journey to higher levels of consciousness, or do you feel that you are stuck somewhere?

Genuine Love Flows from Solidarity with Others

The spiritual journey toward God leads us to be "for" others because God is like the father in the parable of the lost son relentlessly "for" his kids even when they fail (see Lk. 15:11–32). He is like love-struck parents instinctively hatching plans to help their newborn baby thrive. The Good Samaritan displayed this "for-others" heart. And I saw it when as a teenager my father purchased a painting from an artist peddling his mediocre artwork. Dad collected as much money as he could coax from everyone in the house for the purchase, and defended the spending of our pocket money on a dodgy painting. Dad simply said, "He needed a lift in his soul." There was no logical reason, just the heart to be "for" humanity and without expecting anything in return.

God loves to the extent of sacrificing his Son simply because he recognizes value in humanity—that we are "one stock," family, and that we are not regarded as objects over-against God, to which he does good from a distance. Because God has thrown in his lot with us *nothing* can isolate us from his love (see Rom. 8:28–39).

Until we can be "for" humanity and not just for ourselves, the life of love will loom before us like Mount Everest. Can you identify what motivates you to do acts of love?

Genuine Love Is Taking Initiative for the Good of Others

Genuine love is more than fiddling at doing good. We aim to please God by not doing wrong (like physically assaulting people) but fail to take initiative for the well-being of others in the seat next to us who are hurt, angry, or estranged from God. The heart of Jesus broke for the rich young man who came to him with all the religious boxes checked but struggled to participate in God's love for him or others (see Mark 10:17ff).

Do you find yourself falling into this live-and-let-live attitude? What do you think causes this?

Genuine Love Saves and Restores

If following Jesus leads us to God and the good life, then leading other people to be his true followers is one of the supreme expressions of genuine love.

At their final meal together Jesus washes his disciples' feet and commands them to love each other in the same way he has loved them (John 13:34). Importantly, they are to love *each other*, but with the Cross in view "love one another" surely means selfless service bringing about salvation and restoration in the full sense of what his death and resurrection made possible, right? Obviously Jesus didn't lay down his life *only* for his followers but for all who are lost (Lk. 19:10). Genuine love is not about sprinkling people with a topcoat of sugar, but about the heart to participate in a Spirit-empowered war against the powers of darkness that rob people of their sacred identity as loved by God, joy, peace, freedom, health, and ultimately resurrection. More than charity, it is to fight for justice—to put right what is wrong in God's creation. When the "niceness" of Christianity masquerades as love, it demotes the nature of our participation in God's redemptive plan to things that don't matter.

What do you truly want your life to be about?

Genuine Love Is More than Moralizing

As the story unfolds at the end of Luke 11 (vv. 37–54) Jesus takes his seat at the meal table of a Pharisee but contravenes acceptable behavior by failing to first wash his hands. This isn't about hygiene; a bitter debate erupts over an issue clearly of supreme importance to Jesus: *What does it mean to be pure? What attitudes and behaviors please God?*

We should be moral, but Jesus ruthlessly dismantles their misconception that religiously checking the box on hand-washing (or any marginal right-doing) makes you pure or morally acceptable. He tells them how to achieve the purity God is after: *by loving a broken world and giving to the poor.*

Jesus challenges the Pharisees' idea that *moralizing,* or identifying right from wrong, is enough to please God and find his life. Religious hand-washing expresses absolutely nothing of God's heart of love, so how can it create any overlap between the circle of God's life and ours?

Almsgiving in the first century was nothing like our skinny idea of charity today—often offering a handout from a distance. It entailed embracing those in need as if they are members of your own family.[28]

Jesus didn't pontificate on right and wrong from a distance, or stop at good acts such as signing petitions to challenge injustice, or sending money to support poor children. No. He rolled up his sleeves to pray, offer friendship, heal, and reconcile amongst the poor, broken-hearted, sick, lost, guilty, and marginalized as an agent of restoration. *Until we do this life-on-life with others and have some skin in the game are we really much past moralizing?* Thomas Merton wrote:

> Love means an interior and spiritual identification with one's brother, so that he is not regarded as an "object" to "which" one "does good." The fact is that good done to another as to an object is of little or no spiritual value.[29]

This is reinforced later in Luke's narrative (Lk. 12:1–12) when Jesus instructs his disciples to guard against "the yeast of the Pharisees"—that is, *their hypocrisy to appear pious, godly, and spiritual while at the same time sidestepping any real expression of genuine love through compassion, justice, or mercy to those in need.* God always intended his people to bring a time of grace, restoration, and shalom[30] as shown in the Jubilee practice of Israel and expressed in powerfully spiritual ways through the ministry of Jesus. Israel and the Church were always intended to glorify God by embodying his love to heal the world and restore the wholeness of Eden. Ritual hand-washing, arm's-length handouts, and any other sort of marginal right-doing just aren't on this map.

What would motivate you, personally, to embrace Christ's rally-call to love, or conversely to opt for marginal right-doing instead?

Genuine Love Profits Us Spiritually

Paul's stunning words on love (1 Cor. 13) to the Corinthians made the point: even seemingly spiritual or good things without genuine love do not enhance our relationship with God. The sorts of deeds Paul includes, such as providing for the poor, obviously benefit the *recipients*. However, without being characterized by the sort of love described in 1 Corinthians 13:4–7, the *giver's* relationship with God is not enhanced.[31] This is because attitudes and actions inconsistent with genuine love diminish people and, therefore, scream against the sphere where God works and wants to be. It holds then that expressions of genuine love *do* enhance our relationship with God, helping us live in that sphere and come alive spiritually (see also John 15:9–13).

What the saints and mystics called "union with God" was a life transformed by the resurrection of genuine God-grade love in it, and Fenelon's story helps to animate the journey.

Fenelon's Story

François Fenelon was an intellectual genius in France who experienced life-of-love revolution.[32] Fenelon was entrusted with the education of King Louis XIV's heir, and in 1694 was appointed Archbishop of Cambrai. His fame was skyrocketing when he was introduced to Madame Guyon, the French mystic who taught on the crucifixion of the self-life and living a life of pure love, or abandonment to God's will. Her non-anxious embrace of God's will impressed Fenelon, and the life of love became for him like a fine pearl.

Fenelon believed but desired more of God. We can experience a "touch" from God but not be transformed if we resist his will, because our transformation and God's kingdom are expressed in terms of that will (see Matt. 6:10). Fenelon struggled to move beyond selfish habits and self-sufficiency but deeply desired to be transformed to be like Jesus. *It is not our failure to perform but our lack of desire that gets us into spiritual trouble.*

He apparently understood it all intellectually but was sluggish to let God love him. In a letter to Madame Guyon before his own transformation, Fenelon wrote:

> When we have proceeded so far, we may say with a good deal of reason, that the natural man is dead. And then comes, as a fifth step in this process, the NEW LIFE, not merely the *beginning* of a new life, but a new life in the higher sense of the terms, the resurrection of *the life of love.* All those gifts which the soul before sought in its own strength, and perverted and rendered poisonous and destructive to itself, by the seeking them out of God, are now richly and fully returned to it, by the great Giver of all things.
>
> And this life . . . becomes a truly transformed life, *a life in union with God,* when the will of the soul becomes not only conformed to God practically and in fact, but is conformed to Him in everything in it, and in the relations it sustains, which may be called a *disposition* or *tendency.* It is then, there is such a harmony between the human and divine will, they may be properly regarded as having become one. This, I suppose, was the state of St. Paul, when he says, 'I live; yet not I, but Christ liveth in me. . . .'
>
> This transformed soul does not cease to advance in holiness. It is transformed without remaining where it is; new without being stationary. Its life is love, *all* love; but the capacity of that love continually increases.

Fenelon entered and championed this interior life that challenges the self and releases pure love. Along with Madame Guyon and others, Fenelon was accused by self-serving and corrupt priests of teaching heresy. Bishop Bossuet, a literary genius of that day, wrote books to annihilate Fenelon, but Fenelon's replies were so saturated with a spirit of love he won the people's hearts. Eventually, Bossuet appealed to the pope, and the king banished Fenelon to his own diocese of Cambrai where, until his death in 1715, he ministered among Flemish peasants.

Many stories are told of the love of this intellectual genius for these simple country folk. For instance, one day Fenelon met a peasant who was sad because he had lost a cow. He gave the man enough money to buy another cow, but the man was still sad because he really liked the lost cow. Fenelon searched until he found it. The sun had set and it was dark, but he drove the cow all the way back to the peasant's house.

How do you relate to Fenelon's struggle? Think through the ways in which the capacity of God's love is being expressed through your life.

Swings of the Pendulum

Church history shows parts of the church at different times and places circling around a synthesis of the two sides of our paradox rather than finding balance in any lasting way. While this doesn't apply across the board, the insights can sharpen our own spiritual pilgrimage.

By the third century, mass conversions led Constantinople to expediently stop appointing priests to hear confessions, and moral standards in society plummeted.[33] Monasticism with its vital spiritual life and missionary activity was a reaction to this laxity.

However, legalism soon tiptoed back through asceticism, severe self-discipline aimed at pleasing or getting closer to God, and while this was not universally true, the pendulum swung away from grace.

The eleventh and twelfth centuries saw the rise of penance and indulgences in the Catholic Church.[34] These practices continued and grew, then, for another three centuries.

In 1517, Martin Luther dismantled these ideas, teaching salvation as a free gift of God's grace. Thankfully the pendulum swung away from this extreme, but it swung to the opposite extreme. Still today, too many Christians find Luther's God-inspired stance on grace as an excuse for not doing anything much in response to God—at least not anything that is intentional, committed, or costly. Luther himself did not believe we should *remove* works, but rather they should be ripples of the transforming power of God's love in us.[35]

In the first 150 years of the Reformation era, "antinomianism" (meaning "anti-law") threatened.[36] In many cases being freed from the law as a way of salvation was assumed to bring with it freedom from the law as a guide to conduct,[37] allowing selectivity in terms of a practical response to God, and the pendulum swung too far.

German pietism in the seventeenth century championed the idea that God can renew the heart, and this should be evident in expressions of love in everyday life for God's glory and man's good.

In the 1700s, in Great Britain, John Wesley, the founder of the Methodist movement, taught that biblical Christianity must demonstrate its reality in a "faith working by love." He saw individuals as totally sinful and entirely dependent on grace but also free to make choices, "which made a person an active subject with moral obligations."[38] He advocated some sort of response to grace in our Monday-to-Saturday lives. This teaching spawned the holiness movement which, in a reaction to antinomianism, went too far in emphasizing the importance of adhering to the law (the Word of God), thereby losing sight of grace in the synthesis. In the 1970s and 1980s quite legalistic church cultures surfaced with strict moral codes for behavior (albeit amidst an enriching embrace of the work of the Holy Spirit and focus on God's Word).

The 1990s saw an expedient reaction because strict moral codes stopped people from attending church and hindered evangelism, and much of the church gained a fresh appetite for success.[39] Some churches pursuing success at the expense of spiritual depth supplemented the declining spiritual pulse with "doses" of the supernatural.[40] In the New Testament involvement in the supernatural work of the Holy Spirit (spanning the spiritual journey and kingdom works) is normative for believers and transforming. But with surface-doses of it many people seem, like the multitudes milling around Jesus, to still need God's love to permeate deeply enough to be transforming.

The pendulum has swung too far, and sections of the church are reacting to this thinness with talk of "reinventing" the church. Whatever the forms God ordains to take us forward, they will serve what is critical for life with God, and that is a synthesis of our paradox. Think about the pendulum swings in your own journey, and how this helps you move forward.

Wherever we happen to be right now in our journey, to find our way to where the Lamb is, we must stop fighting against a synthesis of the two sides of our paradox and follow him. Our question now is, how?

For Discussion

1. What sort of things have you done to get closer to God?
2. Discuss the idea that love is both integral to life beyond the flatland and a "higher level of consciousness." What does this mean for your personal journey toward God?
3. Do you think you are able to let God love you? Explain. Why is this important?
4. Do you find yourself leaning toward one side or the other of our paradox? How do you think this might diminish your life with God?

5. What is a *life* of love? Share your own experience of the flow of God within you by the Holy Spirit enabling you to encounter and express God's love.

6. Which of the insights about genuine love impacted you the most, and why?

7. What does Fenelon's story show us about how to resurrect the life of love?

8. What insights did you receive for your own spiritual pilgrimage from reading about the pendulum swings between the two sides of our paradox in church history?

PART TWO

Spiritual Dynamics

CHAPTER 3

The Hidden Unwilling

To have found God and still to pursue Him is the
soul's paradox of love, scorned indeed by the too
easily satisfied religionist, but justified in happy
experience by the children of the burning heart.

—A. W. TOZER[41]

We can consider ourselves Christians and can be active participants in church life while being *un*willing for the way of Jesus! Moreover, this unwillingness can even be hidden by the way the church operates.

A pastor was pleased about a ministry in his church feeding thousands in need, and in conversation with the Lord about it, he said, "We're feeding the poor as you have asked." The Lord retorted, "You're right, but paid staff members run the ministry—very few others are feeding the poor simply because I'm their Lord!" The church machine was producing results that dolled up the church to look spiritually healthier than it was in reality. *The spiritual impact of this can be devastating because, under the cover of church "success," its members can be languishing in the spiritual flatland while there is also a misconception that nothing much needs to change.*

Based on hard evidence, do you think you are willing or unwilling for Christ's way?

Heart Audit

We have all crossed paths with genuine followers who look, smell, and act like Jesus in exquisite ways—just not enough to make a critical mass. *Whatever is adopted by a critical mass of Christians will define church life.*

The issue: spiritual dynamics or the effect of church life *on our hearts.* Our church activities might "work" on one level, but a truer spiritual diagnostic requires we audit our heart and ask, "Is our hunger for God rising?" How would you answer this for yourself? *Discipleship isn't primarily about doing a course or having a mentor to learn how to do Jesus-things, but finding passionate desire in our heart for God, his way of love, and his work. Discipleship makes God our oasis and forms Christ in us* (see Gal. 4:19). Beyond external propping for our faith, Christ's life spontaneously flows through us by the Spirit as we find desire and willingness for it.

The key to relating to God is not our proficiency, but to actually *want* a relationship with him. Do you agree? It is the grace to be barefoot. Living in God's kingdom is about doing the will of God from your heart (see Eph. 6:6 and Col. 3:22); both doing his will and doing it willingly does matter. If so, having our unwillingness hidden is a curse, and instead we should chart a spiritual course that *transforms* our will.

The Further Journey

In Robert Burnell's prophetic allegory *Escape from Christendom,*[42] a lone traveler in search of the City of God thinks he has found it when he discovers a bustling metropolis crammed with impressive Christian things such as massive cathedrals. But an ancient man tells the traveler that this is not the City of God; to find it will require a further journey. The ancient man leads him along a narrow, humble path up a mountain, to where the desert begins. He can see the City of God, throbbing like a living thing of unrivalled beauty, but to reach it he must first cross the desert and its four wildernesses: forgiveness, worship, prayer, and the harvest. Where would you place yourself: harboring in "Christian City" or venturing into the desert? Sadly, this journey into the "desert" is starkly different from the default "spirituality" undergirding much of church life today; I will refer to it as "the construct."

In the desert, all is stripped bare, and issues of the heart are forced into the open, making true spirituality possible. John (like Jesus) made a vital connection between living in God's kingdom and doing heart-work.[43]

John portrayed the Lord coming to us on a road built through our hearts, and for him to come the road must be free of obstacles (Lk. 3:4–6). This "roadwork" (or heart-work) involves removing pride, selfishness, self-reliance, and any other hindrance to our involvement in God's redemptive purposes. This baptism of repentance (Lk. 3:2–3) prepares us for baptism with the Holy Spirit and fire (Lk. 3:16).

Many Christians today see repentance as superficially saying "sorry" to get back into God's good books, but with nothing much changing in our everyday lives. Spiritual progress involves leapfrogging over the mere avoidance of wrongdoing and dabbing at sin with a prayer and a goat, to inward reformation by the Holy Spirit energizing us for what is right and pleasing to God (Rom. 12:1–2).

What potholes in your heart require work?

Secret Soul-work

The desert is a powerful biblical symbol of separation and the preparation of the heart for relationship with God. It draws us beyond our self-sufficiency, probing into issues of trust and obedience and, as we see with the biblical Israel, it may result in failure, rebellion, and judgment. Importantly, it moves beyond surface appearances to a person's inner being. *God can't relate to a fabrication.*

The bright lights of Jerusalem's religious system (and there are parallels in the church today) distracted from responses of the heart and, rather than championing the inward change required for right response to God and removing their sandals in reverent response to Christ, the religious leaders ran the show and ultimately killed him.

Jesus fled to the desert to escape the distracting sounds of unfaithful Jerusalem for a fighting chance to discern his Father's voice. We often miss the mystic in Jesus, who involved himself personally in spiritual practices and secret soul-work.

The desert is an invitation to silence, solitude, and waiting on God. Jerusalem, on the other hand, corralled people as religious spectators, thriving on religious consumption and making things happen. The desert offers the mystery of deep calling to deep. Jerusalem had become surface deep. The desert makes you honest about yourself, removing your props and setting you up for a liaison with love. Jerusalem demanded performance and appearances. In the desert, you enter the skin of your identity as God's loved child; sadly, Jerusalem offered a religious treadmill. The desert runs on surrender, Jerusalem on control. The desert births and nurtures desire for God; Jerusalem coerced the unwilling for self-serving ends. In the desert, Christ's mind gained traction, and a new creation jumped from its box; Jerusalem was compulsive like the world. People go to the desert to hear God speak; Jerusalem was for those hankering to win arguments or show off. The desert fosters a community without boundaries with ears for the sacred call to work with God in every corner of creation; in Jerusalem, the office-bearers pushed corporate identity and expectations.

In the desert, we come to understand *nothing* we do can upgrade God's love toward us, but to participate in his life requires consistently doing *something* in positive response to his love.

In what ways do you think you practice desert spirituality?

St. Anthony's Story

St. Anthony, one of the Desert Fathers, was born to Egyptian peasants around 251. In his late teens Anthony withdrew into the desert seeking transformation and lived in solitude for twenty years. *In solitude, we discover the parts of us that are unloved and the parts of us that are unable to love.* As Catholic priest and writer Henri Nouwen writes, we are forced into a faceoff with what is really going on inside us.

> In solitude I get rid of my scaffolding: no friends to talk with, no telephone calls to make, no meetings to attend, no music to entertain, no books to distract, just me—naked, vulnerable, weak, sinful, deprived, broken—nothing. It is this nothingness that I have to face in my solitude a nothingness so dreadful that everything in me wants to run to my friends, my work, and my distractions so that I can forget my nothingness and make myself believe that I am worth something. But that is not all. As soon as I decide to stay in my solitude, confusing ideas, disturbing images, wild fantasies, and weird associations jump about in my mind like monkeys in a banana tree. Anger and greed begin to show their ugly faces. I give long hostile speeches to my enemies and dream lustful dreams in which I am wealthy, influential, and very attractive—or poor, ugly, and in need of consolation. Thus I try again to run from the dark abyss of my nothingness and restore my false self in all its vainglory.[44]

This battle with our demons offers a disconcerting soul-experience, a crucible that accelerates the possibility of unconditional surrender to Jesus. Like a child recovering from a painful fall, we slump, crying, into his arms and open the gates of our soul to his love. The words of Jesus soothe, forgive, heal, reshape, secure. No need now to compete, strive, criticize, or serve ourselves. Again Nouwen writes, "It is in this solitude that we become compassionate people, deeply aware of our solidarity in brokenness with all of humanity and ready to reach out to anyone in need."[45] How do you feel about the idea of solitude, and why?

When Anthony resurfaced from the desert genuine love, compassion, humility, wisdom, powerful miracles, and healings shaped his legend. He powerfully lived out a synthesis of the two sides of our paradox. Anthony spent the end of his life in solitude again to be totally absorbed in God, because God—rather than doing things for God—is our raison d'être.

Anthony's story might seem extreme, but it shows the transforming power of communion with God via the spiritual life. For most, it's unlikely to mean running away to the Sahara, but for anyone hungry for intimacy with God, it must mean assuming responsibility for forming our own desert—seeking our own times of solitude, silence, and prayer. How do you think this could happen in the context of your own life?

The Desert and Spiritual Alertness

To grasp the idea of the desert I am talking about, don't think geographical location. Instead, think of it as a mix of a hungry heart, the right environment, and time allowing us to be alone with God in a way conducive to revelation and spiritual transformation. Saint Anthony didn't seek God in the desert because sand dunes are more holy, but because the solitude and silence of the place were conducive to heart-work and spiritual alertness. He said it this way:

> Just as fish die if they stay too long out of water, so the monks who loiter outside their cells [huts in the desert] or pass their time with men of the world lose the intensity of inner peace. So like a fish going towards the sea, we must hurry to reach our cell, for fear that if we delay outside we will lose our interior watchfulness.[46]

The desert has its trials, but it's not a hard, dry place to be escaped. We should beeline for the desert as a place pregnant with the promise of transformation and the quenching streams of grace. It is not lonely because we bump into God there. It purifies, empowers, and promises to reveal to us the footprints of Jesus and his love. The desert makes us strong and sure about what we hope for by helping us to be both self-aware and God-aware. The desert re-wires our hearts so we can believe, love, rest, and act with joy. It plugs us in spiritually!

The person who takes a day out of hectic busyness or turns off the TV and computer to be still, to listen, to be renewed and pick up the frequency of God's voice again, to pray, has gone to the desert.

This secret soul-work is not just for ancient mystics in monasteries or quirky, "unproductive" people on the fringes. Extreme asceticism in the pendulum swings of church history must not be allowed to devalue life-giving spirituality. Biblically defined spirituality with its desert practices and culture is the lifeblood of kingdom living. It is to a life of faith and pilgrimage in the way of the Lamb, as water is to the sea.

The Construct: Interfering with Spirituality

The antithesis to the desert is the construct: the external structure, activities, and dynamics built around us as motivation to do what the Bible says and to make the church work. The term "construct" is not a blanket description of the church today or a condemnation of structure (which is necessary but must serve spiritual life). Instead it simply identifies spiritual dynamics that make it difficult for Christians to develop a transforming life with God, and we must each assess whether it applies to us or our community. Let me say that my intention here is only to *strengthen* church communities spiritually by clearly identifying these dynamics.

The construct offers a surrogate set of "spiritual" transactions by which we are given what we want, we are entertained, and we feel good in return for attendance and supporting church activities. *The problem is precisely that this sabotages the spiritual life by replacing the spiritual activities and dynamics upon which a transforming life with God is built—immersion in Christ by receiving and responding to his love firsthand.*

At best, this stems from well-intended but ill-informed efforts by leaders to vitalize the church; at worst, from an unhealthy drive on the part of leaders to ensure their church grows in numbers. The notion is confronting, but essentially: *we serve people (even in spiritual ways) to preserve and prosper an organization in which we have vested the power to determine our significance and identity.*

Passive Spectators vs. Real Participants

Construct dynamics leave the critical mass of a church community as "passive spectators"—an audience with very limited real participation or function. Unwilling followers are propped up to ensure results. What a far cry from the transforming honesty of the desert or the vibrant early church communities described in 1 Corinthians 14:26, which thrived on a real contribution from *every* member as they tracked on the heels of Jesus into the life of love! Compromising on the life-giving rigors and mystery of biblical or desert spirituality is an externality of the construct— the price we must pay to keep people coming. But the real cost is forfeiting God's transforming presence.

A friend attended a particular church because it was like going to a theater. He didn't have to do anything; he could come and go "under cover." It was a manageable time commitment, and he enjoyed the services like one would enjoy a Hollywood movie. The consumer was sovereign—a spiritually fatal danger. The kingdom life is made palatable to our busy Western lives with rewards offered, displacing Jesus from front and center. This is sanctioned because it makes the church work, but are our lives rich in God's love and on fire for him?

When construct dynamics take over, church communities can parade false fullness or artificial attractiveness. It is artificial because it flows from human effort rather than God's presence. There exists the subtle but convincing idea its network of activities constitutes the spiritual cosmos, and disengagement risks missing God because he isn't anywhere else. This is leveraged by the sociological dynamic of feeling connected to a "big, powerful thing."[47] However, it can dish up so much ego and group satisfaction it distracts from the search for, and authentic experience of, God.

The most convincing evidence of this is the incredible levels of human effort and external activity necessary to make churches today attractive to people. Also consider the arresting fact Western Christians are not generally considered to be people who love each other. If there isn't much energy or conviction for relating dynamically with God beyond the construct machinery, this is further evidence. On top of all this, research consistently shows many Christians are indistinguishable from non-Christians in important areas of attitude and behavior. Either they have shifted away from a biblical view of life, or they have joined a stream of Christian belief that doesn't ascribe to it or lacks the power to realize it.

Confusing the Messenger with the Messiah

The construct subtly serves itself rather than pointing beyond itself to God. Good things may be happening, but the problem lurks in a different dimension—the heart, and the impact of church activity (good or bad) on our true attitude toward God. There are many wonderful leaders, but this construct dynamic strikes you between the eyes when a leader leaves even the crumbs of an idea that they are in any way messianic, and we gravitate toward them as some sort of messiah. Just think about how often the small talk after a conference or church service pivots around the speaker or worship leader, a daring missionary, someone used by God to heal the sick or prophecy, rather than *God*. Of course God works through people, but what does it do to our life with God if we depend more on *their* prophecies, sermons, exploits, and healing prayers than on God?

Do we give Jesus our uncompromised focus, allegiance, and affection? Small talk after a Sunday service about how great so-and-so was has its place to encourage, but it does reveal a deficiency of the sort of testimony of the Messiah by which everyone and everything else is forgotten. It shows blunt spiritual focus. *The service we offer to God should be forgotten by others, not because we have necessarily served badly but simply because it is of such a lower order of things.*

John knew he was merely the best man at the wedding, not the Bridegroom: he must do his job and slip from the limelight (see John 3:30). John's importance didn't decrease just because of his humility, but because it is a compelling divine necessity—God is in Christ betrothing us to *himself.* Life with God involves being *Christ's* Bride, and for this reason God's servants must do their job and then happily get out of the way so people will cross the river and forge their own spiritual life with the Christ, offering *him* their affection and praise. When the transcendent or heavenly fills the space, the earthly decreases. The greater displaces the lesser. But when we make messiahs of lesser servants because we can't discern the greater King amongst us, this is bad religion because people can't save us.

Some considered John the Baptist could fit the profile of the Messiah (see Lk. 3:15), but he leaves no crumbs that would tip anyone to the notion he was even a great messenger, let alone the Messiah (see Lk. 3:16). He was saying, "Look to Jesus and forget me altogether if you want the kingdom." *The cult of the great messenger is classic construct and it makes the church spiritually weak.*

In recent decades spiritual practice has declined among the critical mass of churchgoers leaving our spiritual life threadbare and weakening our spiritual relationship with the *person* of the transcendent Son of God. Messengers are mere people, and when we depend on them we soon forfeit the fear of God that was evident in the early church but is conspicuous by its absence in the church today (see 2 Cor. 5:11–17). At bedrock, we can take or leave anything we don't like or struggle to accept when spoken by mere people. "You are the apple of God's eye" or "Serve the poor" are easily discarded. However, the instant we discern the transcendent Son of God speaking to us, it is a different matter—the fault lines in our souls shift, we are responsive, our life with God expands.

Confusion about who the Messiah is tempts leaders to compromise their role as a voice in the desert calling for the heart-work that will prepare the spiritual highway upon which King Jesus will come to them (see John 1:23). The spiritually suspect underbelly of the construct pokes into view, and the eternal significance of it echoes in the regretful words of believers when they finally meet the glorious Jesus Christ face-to-face: "I let that person steal my affections from you, and I also lost my vision of you."

Who would you say captures most of your attention—your leaders or Jesus?

The Exaltation and Absorption of the Individual

Construct dynamics further weaken church communities spiritually by elevating the individual to the center of things in place of God. *Sure, there is worship, the preaching of God's Word, and other God-things, but it must all be to the liking of the individual.* The convenience of individuals must be served and pathways provided upon which they can rise to significance or reach their desired destiny. The construct declares the individualistic vision that God will exalt *me* rather than the biblical vision of glimpsing the glory of God. At bedrock, "What do people want?" challenges the question "What does God want?" Sometimes this is overt and sometimes subtle, but it is quintessential construct thinking that is entrenched because it keeps people filing through the doors. Of our own lives and of any community of faith we should ask,

"Beyond what is spoken and obvious, is the individual usurping the place of exaltation that belongs exclusively to God?"

Full-blown individualism is woven into the fabric and heartbeat of Western society today: *the valuing above all else of the expression of an individual's own identity, desires, independence, self-sufficiency, control over others and the universe, and goals as a means to their ultimate life potential.* It has also seeped into church life, and this poses a problem: in the New Testament, the ultimate experience of life and God occurs as the *opposite* of individualism—in our need for others in accountable and supportive community, and placing God rather than the individual front and center.

In John's apocalyptic vision of heaven on the island of Patmos, God's redeemed people press in as a community around his throne with a no-compromise concentration upon God and the Lamb: "Salvation belongs to our God, who sits on the throne, and to the Lamb" (Rev. 7:10). Those experiencing salvation are in no doubt *God* and his exploits are of prime importance, not the needs or deeds of individual people. The Revelation 7 community understood this doesn't mean God neglects people, but rather that when he is at the center, he will address all of their needs.

> . . . they stand in front of God's throne
> and serve him day and night in his Temple.
> And he who sits on the throne
> will give them shelter.
> They will never again be hungry or thirsty;
> they will never be scorched by the heat of the sun.
> For the Lamb on the throne
> will be their Shepherd.
> He will lead them to springs of life-giving water.
> And God will wipe every tear from their eyes
> (Rev. 7:15–17).

We should declare a holy fast from our dependence on what men and women can do for us. Instead, engage in an uncompromised pursuit of what *God* is saying to us and what *God* wants to do in and through us with the fervor and urgency of revolutionaries. We should fight for our church communities to be places where people are known personally, loved genuinely, and empowered for a transforming life with God, rather than just indulged *en masse*.

There is a second perversion to do with individuals: they are put to work to ensure construct goals are achieved. They must attend, give financially, invite friends, and participate in small groups and other cogs in the corporate wheel. *Are individuals serving the construct or God—corporate aspirations or the sacred calling to unleash their gifts and uniqueness creation-wide for God's glory?* With paid professionals assigned the key functions of ministry, rank-and-file individuals are left doing spiritual drone work that limits the flow of God's life through them to what seems like a trickle from a tap.

Spiritual Tasks vs. Spiritual Practice

Any activity that concentrates us on God and receiving his love, in examining our conscience and in exercising or training our hearts to make room for his Word, in hearing his voice, and responding obediently—is spiritual practice. *In effect, it is a workout for our hearts and lives in the liberating rhythms of Christ's life.*[48] These activities, called spiritual practices, exercises, or disciplines, are structured ways of connecting us relationally with God. Without our own rhythm of spiritual practice, we will struggle to find God or grow. This is how it works:

> In practice, each spiritual exercise is a holy desire, a sacred seed. The Spirit, working through the exercise, plows and turns the earth of my life to make me ready for God. I plant the seed, the Lord grows it in secret, and the Creator brings forth a hundredfold harvest (see Matt. 13:24–30, 36–43).[49]

Spiritual practice facilitates a life-giving and dynamic corre-spondence with God—receiving and responding—bread and butter to the desert life and to Christian spirituality. Of course, our engagement with God (and experience of salvation) on earth will fall short of the Revelation 7 or heavenly version because the impurity of our hearts blurs our vision of God (see Matt. 5:8). But the invitation is no less wonderful, and the importance of spiritual practice is clear.

Spiritual tasks, on the other hand, are spiritually oriented activities that merely serve earthbound expectations (from us and others). *The distinction between "task" and "practice" boils down to the motivation for our activity.* We might pore over the Bible, be the pillar of corporate prayer meetings, or serve at the Saturday outreach, all because we feel under pressure to earn brownie points with God or want to be noticed by others (spiritual task), and not do these things as an expression of hunger for God and of holy fear (spiritual practice). Are your spiritual activities more task or practice?

Constructs push commitment to spiritual tasks to keep the wheels turning; encouraging true spiritual practice threatens its professionalism and no-inconvenience appeal. The issue: *we can be highly committed to doing spiritual tasks but remain spiritually flat.*

Colin Marshall and Tony Payne, in *The Trellis and the Vine*, [50] employ the helpful image of a garden trellis and a vine to make the point: trellis-work (or building up the support structures and activities of the church: the construct) tends to take over from vine-work (or the work of helping people to grow spiritually: desert practices). And without vine-work the New Testament vision of mature disciples, reproducing themselves by preaching the gospel in the power of the Holy Spirit, is a pipe dream.

After erecting a superb trellis for some soon-to-be planted snow peas, I realized that until I grew the snow pea vines, there would be no food to eat! Hordes of believers attend church but don't eat or grow, and the telltale signs appear in the pulse of their lives *beyond* the boundaries of the construct. We might be jumping out of our skin at church activities, but struggle to find God or share the gospel on our own time.

Church life must help us grow *spiritually*, and this involves "not just ministry skills and competencies, but growth in convictions (understanding) and character (godliness)."[51] It must help us hear God speak and involve our lives in a transforming way with the Holy Spirit. This is how the kingdom comes, not just by association with the trellis.

The Pursuit of Success vs. Wholeness

God sent his Son so we can be *whole*, but the construct manages its transactions with people to prioritize its own *success*. Let me offer some examples. A success model can depend on expediently welcoming and connecting people, but wholeness involves deep friendship and healing through the acceptance and love of authentic community. Construct success hinges on using people for church jobs, but wholeness involves empowering people to jump into their sacred God-life using their gifts. Shallow leaders fascinate people with their revelation, but wholeness-centered leaders humbly guide others to receive their own revelation. To succeed, we treat dull people like children, telling them what to do and offering external incentives to ensure the corporate result. Toward wholeness, we call people to accountability and responsibility and to walk in the journey of growth—we appreciate the sacredness of life, the power of love, and the presence of God.

After careful thought, would you opt for wholeness or success as the priority for your faith community?

The Lost Stream

Let me tell a simple little story to help us step back from the details and come to grips with the bigger picture. A seemingly insignificant stream dribbled along behind a village. Legend ascribed life-giving powers to its water. The forefathers rummaged through jungle undergrowth to locate the hidden stream bubbling from a deep spring, and then they would kneel and drink. The journey was hot and the flies pesky, but their thirst was quenched.

When civilization came to the village, the people became tired of rummaging through the jungle in the heat for water. A shop was built selling soda pop, and the stream was forgotten. The buzz around the village was about progress. The shop was doing a roaring trade, but everyone remained strangely thirsty.

This paints a vivid picture of the spiritual outfall when we become tired of reaching for the hidden, deep-flowing stream of God's love, grace, and power revealed by the Holy Spirit (see 1 Cor.12:13). *Without the energy to find the stream or the humility to kneel and drink, we cannot receive anything from God.* No love, forgiveness, healing words, vision, truth, hope, peace, spiritual authority, or power; no receiving, no response, no authentic life with God.

The construct masquerades as the embodiment of progress, appealing to "easily satisfied religionists" but without the spiritual power to quench the thirst of their souls.

Like the challenges intrepid adventurers face to unlock the final vault leading to the Holy Grail, reaching this lost stream has a challenge too: its water is found in the desert, and each person must find it for themselves. Is it possible we have, at the door to the last vault, balked at this foolish idea? Have we been put off by the fact the Stream starts so hidden and small and personal? Is it possible we have built scaffolding over the Stream, effectively replacing it with a shop peddling a plethora of sugary drinks that do not satisfy?

Time to Be Honest

At some point, I decided to trade being a proud manager for the calling of spiritual leadership. Of course, a host of questions flooded in on the heels of my decision. What would happen if we challenged construct dynamics? Would it help to infuse the vine with God-life? How do we move forward?

In our fellowship, we pumped time, energy, and resources into convincing ourselves of what we supposedly already believed. We evangelized the evangelized, converted the converted *again*—did we miss something the first time? We exhorted, gave permission, envisioned, and even co-opted grace as a motivator for discipleship. Afraid of silence, we crammed our community life with words, busy activity, and religious entertainment.

Honestly speaking, this was ultimately aimed at numerical growth by making Jesus a more attractive proposition. An unholy relationship existed between our efforts and the responses of people—an unsanctified meddling with the will. Roles offering significance, novelty, spiritual experiences, anointed preachers, and even opportunities to be charitable to the poor were construct devices to cajole Christians to be "Christian." *To put the brakes on such external motivators would reveal the shocking truth about our level of willingness.*

For years, I felt guilty and un-pastoral for viewing people this way. God's dearly loved children are victims. Identifying unwillingness is not a moral judgment or a labeling of people as "bad." It simply understands that if we make decisions or behave in certain ways, we will experience certain outcomes in life. For example, if we don't engage with God's Word consistently, we cannot expect its truth to set us free. This can only be about serving the release of God's blessing, purpose, and divine design for a life.

The task of true spiritual leadership is to identify the hidden unwilling and lovingly coach them to find God's will in their own hearts. It is to midwife the birth of a spiritual life and a new Spirit-fashioned heart, by which they stand "barefoot" before God—graced with the readiness to follow the Lamb into love and the Father.

Would you welcome or resist this sort of leadership? Why?

Followers with Twisted Arms

The church success culture tempts our leaders to produce "results." Loving, well-intentioned leaders can do arm-twisting inadvertently through intrinsically good things, thereby propping up unwillingness instead of overcoming it by pointing to the spiritual life. The tragedy is Christ's way of love is the way of the truly willing; the pseudo willingness of external motivations is not the same.

For example, a pastor discovered Sarah and her family came to church only when he visited them. I'm not decrying pastoral visits but simply questioning arm-twisting surrogates for an intrinsic willingness for God. A church of arm-twisted Sarahs is different in every dimension from a church of Sarahs with an appetite for God.

Moving on, a couple attends church X, but shows little interest in attending a small group. They transfer to church Y, and because they are offered a leadership role in a small group, they become enthused about being in community. Their arms have been twisted, and they will stay as long as they are leading a group.

Next, Bob attends a small church struggling to meet its budget to provide for the needs of pastors in a developing nation. He is not moved to contribute. He transfers to a church with a multimillion-dollar mission budget and is suddenly enthusiastic about being a part of raising a million dollars for missions. The scope of the enterprise has twisted Bob's arm. The real question is whether it has circumvented his heart.

Of course, people can grow when offered a leadership role; they can be prompted to give more when surrounded by acts of generosity. The issue is whether church life is being fueled by external motivations or spiritual enlightenment and growth. How tempting to orient ministry around people's desires because it produces results—whether through short services, Mother's Day gifts, special speakers, novel cutting-edge expressions of church, or even packaged displays of the transcendence of God. Do you need your arm twisted to follow Jesus?

If the Holy Spirit builds the church, why does it seem so dependent on human effort? The answer should be obvious: because our spiritual life is skinny.

Jesus Let Many Walk Away

Jesus didn't do any arm-twisting. He presented himself, offered an invitation to follow, and hit the road again. A stunning example is the story of the rich young man (see Mk. 10:17–22). Jesus loved him enough to arrest his words, but then let him stroll away because he lacked the enlightenment to be a willing disciple. *Jesus was obviously after a motivation to follow from the heart—essential equipment to go beyond our ideas about religion to where Jesus was going.*

Playing spiritual director to guide the young man to a deeper spiritual life meant sacrificing the immediate result—Jesus didn't recruit a follower. Convincing the man to hang around would have been a snap for Jesus because of his authoritative teaching and miracles. But he would need to keep winning the young man over by producing the "goods" to compensate for his unwillingness. Jesus obviously didn't see this as discipleship at all and resisted the temptation to control or exploit him using construct dynamics.

The alternative was internal: the way of the desert and heart. It demanded time and space for the Holy Spirit's soul-work to liberate him to discern Jesus, welcome his terms, and follow willingly. God's presence and the well-being of his soul were at stake, and with extravagant love, Jesus held his line.

This point is echoed in the parable Jesus told about a son who rejects his home and father (see Lk. 15:11–31). Eventually destitute, he lands a job feeding pigs; sobered by the degradation of the pig pens, the son "came to his senses" (Lk. 15:17), realizing he would be better off at home with his father. Energized by fresh "sense," he willingly *runs* home. His father has always loved him, but now the son is powerfully aware of it. His older brother is angry, demanding of the father, "Why don't you love me that way?" The father pleads,

"I have always loved you," but the older brother is blind to it. Self-righteousness is keeping him "senseless" and lacking the passion to run to his father—yet the brother is estranged from the father *at home!* His is the danger of never being found because he hasn't noticed that he is lost—the spiritual peril of indifference when Christ knocks because we are fine without him. Jesus won't force the door. He will give time and space for heart-work until we "come to our senses."

Heeding the Dynamics below the Waterline

Ignoring the dynamics that make us the "hidden unwilling" is like ignoring the rising seawater below the decks of the *Titanic*. Churches today under the influence of construct dynamics present a view of the world like those in the ballroom oblivious to the danger faced by passengers below decks. These sacred communities ignore the spiritual dynamics that threaten danger. The discerning question from the lower decks is: *what is happening to our hearts as a result of church life?*

Transitioning from construct to desert dynamics makes you feel as though you are just keeping your head above water. Initially, transformation and liberation seem slow and beyond our control, but dumbing down the need for heart-work only harbors our unwillingness. Instead, desert culture and practices must be recovered as normal for our church communities if we are to find God's love and cultivate hunger for his will. Then we will be like Tozer's "children of the burning heart" who, having found God, continue to pursue him still, and live in deep, sacred ways.

The next three chapters explore some "don't-leave-home-without-them" spiritual dynamics that are non-negotiable if we are serious about a life of willingness before God: namely, coming to God, corresponding dynamically with him, and discovering our sacred life through discipleship.

For Discussion

1. In your experience, are the "hidden unwilling" a reality? If so, explain how you think it impacts: (1) your own spiritual experience, and (2) the church functioning as a pervasive kingdom force.

2. What is it about the desert life that makes it true spirituality? How does John the Baptist's "baptism of repentance" shed light on this issue?

3. Reflecting on Saint Anthony's story, discuss some practical ways in which you could form your own desert that would be conducive to times of solitude, silence, and prayer.

4. What is the "construct" (discuss some of its main characteristics), and how does it interfere with spirituality?

5. To what extent do you think the church today is influenced by construct dynamics? If they were removed, what do you think would happen?

6. What does the story of the rich young man and the parable of the lost son tell us about why Jesus let many walk away? Discuss the following statement: "Discipleship isn't primarily about doing a course or having a mentor to learn how to do Jesus-things, but finding passionate desire in our heart for God, his way, and his work."

7. What do you personally see as the challenges of transitioning from "construct" to "desert" dynamics?

CHAPTER 4

"Come to Me"

Come to me, all of you who are weary
and carry heavy burdens, and I will give you rest.
Take my yoke upon you and learn from me . . .
and you will find rest for your souls.

—MATTHEW 11:28–29 (NLT)

Life with God kicks off when we are willing to "come" to him. What does that really mean? It is more of a seismic shift in our hearts than just saying we believe in Jesus. It means cranking open our hearts to God and his magnificent Christ-love in such a way that we welcome his authority, voice, and lifestyle in the outward expression of our lives.

The Most Significant Thing a Christian Does

The New Testament writers, and Jesus himself, understood the restoration and salvation Isaiah prophesied would be fulfilled in the Christ. The Father would break into human experience, and the powers of the coming age would be released, through Christ. *The message of the Gospels is that "coming" to or opening our hearts to Christ is the decisive movement toward kingdom reality.* If so, "coming" continually to God in Christ is the most significant thing we can do to find the reality of God. We must start there, keep going back there, and always go back there.

In Matthew 11:28–29 Jesus offers his hearers a real, inner rest: rest for their souls. Two prerequisites for finding this kind of rest jump out at us. First, the invitation targets those who are frazzled because of issues involving religion and life. This is because it is only when we are at the end of our rope that we will "come" to him. Second, we must be prepared to be yoked to him—submitted to his authority and ready to learn from him with the sort of trust that places the ordering of our lives on the line.

Building Our Understanding

To come to him isn't a physical action, but rather a directing of our heart toward Jesus and how we relate to him *inwardly*. Do we need him, trust him, and submit to his authority? Are we "barefoot"?

The Bible—and particularly the teaching of Jesus—teems with insight into this spiritual dynamic that both instigates and perpetuates a deeper connection with God.

The Gospels are brimming with stories about people who seemed all wrong but received forgiveness or healing. Their secret: desperate need blessed them with the grace to submit at heart level to Jesus. Examples include Zacchaeus (Lk. 19:1–10), blind Bartimaeus (Mk. 10:46–52), and the sinful woman who ran to Jesus while he dined with Simon the Pharisee (Lk. 7:36–50).

Probably a prostitute by vocation, this woman enters Simon's house like a contagious disease. Her actions are scandalous—she lets down her hair and fondles his feet as a prostitute would. All of this points to what is *wrong* with her past life, and Simon rams the point home. But Jesus sees her differently: yes, the woman does have a litany of sins, but her recognition of them and her desperation empowers her to "come." Scurrying to Jesus under these circumstances with extravagant expressions of love powerfully parallels her inward "coming," her dependence on grace. She doesn't cower in her failure, pretend she hasn't failed, or give up on being better. No. Having "come" to Jesus for forgiveness, she now keeps "coming," running to him as an act of worship and submission to his guidance about God's will. She yields control, and with trusting acceptance runs to the Light and votes for holiness. *We never run to Jesus and stay where we are; God loves us too much to leave us there.*

In stark contrast, the Pharisees' outward lack of courtesy to Jesus belies their self-righteous attitude. Jesus is at his subversive best here, the consummate spiritual director with keen insight into the spiritual life: *it is not when we are tempted or even when we downright fail that we are in spiritual trouble, as much as when we stop running to Jesus.*

This is resoundingly good news, because temptation, trials, and failure aren't that far removed from even seasoned followers and deeply loved children of God. We can hide behind false appearances for a while, but outward decoration doesn't stamp out what we allow to lurk in the deep recesses of our hearts—attitudes screaming blue murder against God's will. Some sins are out in the open, such as those of this sinful woman, or overt anger, or hurtful actions. Other sins are of the heart—they are hidden, but we are conscious of them: unforgiveness, self-promotion, envy, a critical spirit, self-pity, fear, doubt, self-reliance, and pride. Still other sins are those of *omission*—perhaps we haven't done wrong, but we have failed to do something right; we have carelessly ignored something God prompted us to do, or neglected a central theme of Christ's teaching.

But, if we can honestly recognize what is wrong as this sinful woman did, the wonderful opportunity is afforded us to "come" to Jesus—to run toward grace, light, and holiness. Astoundingly, from what is wrong, God liberates us to run *to him.*

The point resonates also in the parable Jesus told about a tax collector and a Pharisee at prayer in the temple (see Lk. 18:9–14). The Pharisee openly crowed about his list of righteous deeds, but the spiritual prize was awarded to the tax collector who humbly admitted his moral shortfall and sought God's mercy.

So what's wrong with being right as a way to God? First, unlike "coming," punishing ourselves to do right is oppressive. Second, despite how much we suppress sin or know the Bible we are *not* right. The failure of the Pharisee was to blindly claim his innocence when God's view of the human heart is of a twisted, dark, sinful, mess.[52] The tax collector was no worse—or better—than the Pharisee, just more open to the truth.

The irony is identifying with what is *wrong* in us brings loving acceptance and rest from Christ, not a whip. Pinpointing sin elicits hope because "God's law was given so that all people could see how sinful they were. But as people sinned more and more, God's wonderful grace became more abundant" (Rom. 5:20 NLT). The old Puritans prayed for "the gift of tears" so as not to forget how to be sorry for what is not right and forgo the transforming kindness of God. This is the crux of "coming."

Why is owning up to wrong so spiritually powerful? Love is not radical to our soul if we think we are self-right—it is merely justice or what we deserve. Self-rightness immunizes us against passion. However, when we realize the wrong in us, the force of mercy or undeserved goodness that characterizes Christ's love explodes in the corridors of our heart restoring well-being and catalyzing adoration for God. Even down in the bunkers of our soul where our will is well dug in and our sense of inadequacy festers, there is no shelter from this sort of blast.

Turning Our Faces Toward God

A blustery wind whipped up the water at Ella Beach in Port Moresby, Papua New Guinea's capital city. A family was shouting frantically as they searched for their young boy. He had been seen swimming off the rocky outcrop protruding into the bay, but hours had passed now without sign of him. My prayers for them were interrupted within minutes as the ocean seemed to push the boy's lifeless body into view on the beach in front of me. As hysteria and grief gripped the family and the boy was taken away in an ambulance, I sat numbed by the witness of lost life and the family's utter hopelessness.

Then God spoke, reminding me of King David's prayer recorded in Psalm 5:3: "In the morning, LORD, you hear my voice; in the morning I lay my requests before you and wait expectantly." David's circumstances no doubt stretched him, too, but his prayer showed that inwardly, at the core of things, he was oriented toward God—he had come. The insight encourages us, in the midst of a world often shrouded in darkness and beyond explanation, to live from the heart and to find hope by coming to the Light. I felt propelled to inwardly "turn my face" toward God. With the inward shift Godward—looking to, listening, making room, depending, questioning, trusting, and expectantly ready for God's voice—his strength and guidance flew to me on the wings of grace.

"Lift up Your Heads, You Gates!"

When Israel re-enacted the processional carrying the ark through the gates of Jerusalem to the temple, they would sing antiphonally, "Lift up your heads, you gates; lift them up, you ancient doors, that the King of glory may come in. Who is he, this King of glory? The LORD Almighty—he is the King of glory" (Ps. 24:9–10).

King David saw in this ancient liturgy the way God would express his kingship over Israel. The imagery is simple but striking: if a gatekeeper doesn't look toward, embrace, attend to, and welcome the one who approaches, he can't come in. How often the busyness and burdens of life distract us when God approaches our gates. How often we talk him up as the King of Glory, but then treat him like a stranger at the gate. God is already graciously approaching our spiritual gate or heart, and it is our reception of him there—our open-armed welcome and the trusting intent of our gaze like that of David at morning prayers—that give God presence, voice, and authority inside the gate of *our* lives. This way God becomes *our* King, and it profoundly captures the essence of Christian spirituality.

Israel was "napping," and this ancient liturgy was to rouse them to swing their gates wide open by attending to God. The apostle Paul taught: wake up spiritually in this manner and *Christ will shine on you* (Eph. 5:14). Jesus sketched a picture of himself knocking at our spiritual door, teaching that when we come inwardly to attend to him there and welcome his kingship, he will visit us in an intimate way (see Rev. 3:20). The indwelling of Christ is central to Christian theology, but this little piece of mysticism from Jesus shows us how it springs into our real experience. "Lift up your heads, you gates!"

This may seem alien to believers today if we haven't been taught to use our hearts—to converse with God without words. Is heart-talk a part of your relationship with God? A. W. Tozer described faith as the continuous gaze of a soul upon God, and, in return, God would pay attention to the gazing soul. Living outwardly is our school and work mode, but relating spiritually to God requires a taxing shift to live inwardly from the heart. It's like learning to shift the weight of a heavy load from our back to our legs. It requires determined effort, but with mastery comes revolution because the King of Glory can come in!

What is required is the work in the gap. If our lifestyle doesn't welcome the authority and way of the King of Glory (impulsive responses to moments of inspiration aside), we should not wonder why he seems beyond our gates.

Coming Attitudes

In his mountaintop sermon, Jesus taught the wonderful truth that *God desires to bless people*, and certain attitudes invite the kingdom by allowing us to receive his blessing or gifts of goodness. In other words, *God can release his blessing when we are ready to come and to be involved with him in the ways described by these heart-attitudes.* They form the basics of being barefoot, allowing our hearts to come close to God rather than languishing at a distance. In this sense, the Beatitudes in Matthew 5:1–12 are a list of coming attitudes and a treasure trove of insight for pilgrims hungry to learn how to "come" to God. Let's try to get a taste for each of these attitudes.

When we are *"poor in spirit"* (Matt. 5:3), we are deeply aware that we can't make it without God. Now, if we are desperate enough for God, can you see how this attitude would genuinely change our inward disposition toward him? It might for example shift our focus from whatever else makes us busy to an all-out quest to immerse our lives in God and his kingdom—to pray, to listen, to reach for him with our hearts, and to serve him practically. And Jesus-wisdom tells us that seeking means finding (see Matt. 7:8). When the pupil is ready, the teacher appears. The blessing released by this attitude (and otherwise clogged up by attitudes of self-righteousness or self-sufficiency) is the experience of the power and goodness of God's rule.

The attitude of *mourning* (Matt. 5:4) isn't about bereavement; it's about the sorrow of repentance.[53] Unlike the way of most modern pleasure-seekers, it is to grieve over what is wrong in ourselves and our world—poverty, suffering, abused children, refugees, personal sin that injures us and others—and to plead for God's mercy. Mourners "come" by a reorientation toward holiness and love instead of sin. Our blessing—to be bursting with hope that God is addressing our grief as his kingdom comes now, and ultimately when he smashes every last vestige of evil causing his creation pain (see Rev. 21:4).

Meekness (Matt. 5:5) refers to an attitude of submission to the authority of Christ, just as he submitted to his Father in confronting the Cross. A battle of wills no longer exists, but instead an inward strength, conviction of faith, and beautiful obedience permitting Jesus to have his way in our lives. God expresses his kingdom in terms of his will—the meek and not the self-assertive will have a place in it.

When we *"hunger and thirst for righteousness"* (Matt. 5:6), our hearts "come" close to God's heart as a natural by-product of hungering after and loving what he loves. The Holy Spirit has our full cooperation—an unrestricted license—to make us righteous, forming Christ's life in us and in this way satisfying our appetite and our soul.

The *"merciful"* (Matt. 5:7) "come" close to God by choosing to express his heart of mercy as a response to his love. On the heels of our consistent compassion and kindness for others in need, God will also shower us with mercy because it is part and parcel of the economy of love in which we have placed ourselves by our "coming."

To be *"pure in heart"* (Matt. 5:8) means getting things right in our inner lives. Jesus demanded inner purity but taught the human heart is a squirming hotbed of evil (see Matt. 15:19). Because this will be true until Jesus returns, perhaps "coming" by being pure in heart includes the integrity to truly *want* to be pure-hearted. It encompasses authentic pilgrimage toward holiness, risk-taking, and vulnerability for the sake of change, being truly accountable, inviting correction, confessing sins, and remaining humble and teachable. This purifying integrity blesses us with eyes to "see" God—to experience his goodness in close fellowship. Ultimately this blessedness manifests when Jesus returns, evil is no more, and "we shall be like him, for we shall see him as he is" (1 John 3:2). [54]

"Peacemakers" (Matt. 5:9) don't merely *keep* the peace by not rocking the boat, appeasing or avoiding disputes, but work at *making* peace by ending hostilities and bringing conflicting parties together. [55] As peacemakers, we transcend fear and self-preservation to proactively participate in Christ's reconciling work (see Eph. 2:14–18). Our blessing is to know our sacred identity—our place in God's family as his dearly loved children and heirs of everything he possesses (see Gal. 4:3–7). Our souls and lives are secured, anchored in hope.

When we are *"those who are persecuted"* (Matt. 5:10), we have demonstrated our willingness to be insulted, rejected, disgraced, or slandered because we follow Jesus and serve his cause. This is not suffering for doing evil but for being faithful to God [56] *and full of his love.* This attitude enables us to take risks to proclaim and demonstrate the kingdom. And if we are up to our teeth in the work Jesus commissioned his followers to do,[57] we should expect powerful Holy Spirit help and the kingdom to come. "*Because* the Lord has commissioned us to ravish the hearts of the poor with God's goodness, the Holy Spirit is upon us to enable us as we put our hands to that task" (Isa. 61:1a, my paraphrase).

Integral to the manifesto of Jesus on how to find God's good life, these "coming" attitudes form a progressive sequence of the Immersed Life marking an exhilarating spiritual journey into the kingdom heartland:

- being "poor in spirit" is the kingdom gateway through dependence on God;
- "mourning" is a response to seeing the holiness of Jesus—a repentant moment of turning toward him and his stunning heart that stirs passion for God and his kingdom;
- this passion liberates us to be "meek" or to submit to the authority of Christ and worship him without reserve;
- the floodgate then swings open in terms of our responsiveness, making way for the subsequent beatitudes, which are all attitudes in response to grace: longing for what God wants, being merciful, pursuing holiness with integrity, making peace, and being prepared to suffer for God's cause.

CHRIST'S PROGRESSIVE SEQUENCE OF "COMING" ATTITUDES

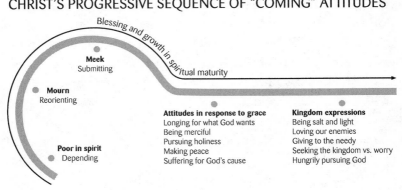

FIGURE 2

Notice it takes this sort of attitudinal progression and maturity before we naturally embrace the kingdom expressions expounded by Jesus in the remainder of his sermon: being salt and light (see Matt. 5:13–16); loving your enemies (see Matt. 5:43–48); giving to the needy (see Matt. 6:1–4); seeking first the kingdom rather than worrying (see Matt. 6:25–34); and hungrily pursuing God (see Matt. 7:7–12). *In other words, spiritual maturity is a progression of inner qualities leading to outward expressions in our lives that please and serve God.* While we will always be revisiting earlier steps in the sequence—for example, to reconnect with our need for God or to submit to Christ's authority in a specific area of our lives—there is a general sense in which we are growing to more naturally embrace each step.

Jesus clearly taught that our inner attitude toward him liberates us to be responsive to him (see John 15:13–15)[58]— not just learning about him or doing things for him, but "coming" to him.

Where would you place yourself in the progression of "coming" attitudes, and which attitudes do you think hold you back spiritually?

What Should We Do?

Our flatness is not because God no longer blesses us or knocks on the door of our heart, and perhaps we have a true desire for God. The issue is a spiritual life gasping for breath without the practices that shape in us the sorts of attitudes allowing us to come to God, eat with him, and receive his blessing. Our insights into what it means to come offers bite-sized opportunities for doing some heart-work to develop these attitudes.

We can't force-feed "coming" attitudes to our souls; to try, ironically, risks self-righteousness that violates what it means to "come." The response of people in the Gospels to Christ is wrapped up in the mysteries of the heart and God's work there. Desperate times were the vehicle of grace for some, freeing their hearts to sprint Godward. This wasn't true for others. For some, success, power, and pride exiled their hearts far from God, but others who had power, such as Nicodemus, found the grace to come. Multitudes experienced God's power tangibly but with hearts in another galaxy from God. Many others were healed by Jesus and gave him their allegiance.

But Jesus establishes what is true for everyone: we encounter God and his goodness when we change *inwardly* and become different sorts of people with different attitudes toward him and others. Jesus champions inner metamorphosis as a pathway to peace, happiness, and collaboration with God to restore a world for which trouble is a reality until he victoriously returns.

If we are open to the soul-work that shapes these attitudes in us, what is our part in it? *First, we can ask God to give us a heart for him and the life of love.* We could, for example, turn the two greatest commandments from Matthew 22:37–39 into a prayer of desire.

Second, we can order our lives so his Spirit has a fighting chance in us. As with setting the formwork into which concrete will be poured, we can take the responsibility of engaging in spiritual practices that pry open the doors of our soul for the Holy Spirit to do the heavy lifting—to reveal our need and the sprawling dimensions of Christ's love[59] freeing us to come. We also give the Spirit a chance to enlighten and grow our heart when we do things in response to God's Word that challenge and stretch its boundary. For example, we can choose from a standing start to forgive, to honor someone else rather than promote ourselves, to give financially to the needy, or to sit quietly to hear God speak rather than spending time on Facebook or stressing over a problem.

The Gift of Destitution

The illusion we don't need God is the ultimate hindrance to coming to him. We falsely believe we can deal with our own pain, find happiness and peace, control the universe, and deal with death. To prop up the delusion, we project to others that we have no pain or fear (even when our souls are a bloody battlefield) and maintain a happy face (even if we feel miserable). Suggestions that we are weak, wounded, wrong, needy, or have failed are offensive in today's religious culture that is all about winning and where winners are the prime candidates for the kingdom. Richard Rohr challenges this notion:

> Truth is more likely to be found at the bottom and the edges of things than at the top or center. The top or center always has too much to prove and too much to protect. I learned this by connecting the dots of the Judeo-Christian Scriptures, from my Franciscan background—the pedagogy of the oppressed and the continued testimony of the saints and mystics—and from the first step of Alcoholics Anonymous. Final authority in the spiritual world does not tend to come from any agenda of success but from some form of suffering that always feels like the bottom.[60]

Eugene Petersen, too, makes the point that the record of King David's failures in the Bible is "not a warning against bad behavior but a witness . . . to the normalcy, yes, the inevitability of imperfection"[61] for those on the Jesus way toward God.

Recognizing our imperfection and destitution, or lack of necessary resources for life, is a gift impelling us to look beyond ourselves to God and his love. The illusion we don't need God is fueled by the deception we can find happiness and peace by meeting the demands of our ego. By being the best, bigger, liked, recognized, beautiful, strong, and known for something, we can find significance and scuttle our deep feelings of inadequacy. But God inspires a life founded in the creative freedom and rest of *already being loved.* Honesty about our insecurity and inadequacy frees us from the soul drive to earn God's love, and his call to obedience doesn't smack of performance to us anymore—it is now a natural part of the new way of living in love that is the Jesus way. *We are able to hear and respond to God's voice calling us to genuinely new ways of thinking and acting.* This is the engine room of transformation and revolution. But God can't change us until hardship, failure, or some other type of "wound" uncovers the no-holds-barred truth about ourselves and the illusion of our self-sufficiency.

From his cross-cultural research on male initiation rites, Richard Rohr identifies five consistent lessons[62] aimed at helping initiates to die to the illusion about their identity and to discover who they really are:

1. Life is hard.
2. You are not that important.
3. Your life is not about you.
4. You are not in control.
5. You are going to die.

Initiates are nudged into liminal space beyond their coping threshold by these truths. The goal is for them to have a numinous encounter and the self-discovery to allow deceptions about themselves and their world to die. Do these five truths highlight corresponding deceptions in your own life?

Across time and cultures, people have consistently realized we need help beyond ourselves, and realizing our destitution is a key to reaching for it. We try to dig out the grit of sand spoiling our illusion, rather than allow it to bring us a pearl—a new way of being in the life of love. Christ brings hope and life to each desta-bilizing truth through the message of his life:[63]

1. Life is hard, *but* we can bear the darkness and find peaceful rest and joy in God's love;
2. You are not that important, *but* your name is already written in heaven;
3. Your life is not about you, *but* God wants to live his life glo-riously through you;
4. You are not in control, *but* God is, so trust him; and
5. You are going to die, *but* because of God's love in Christ, death is not final.

Talking to older saints, you soon realize the secret of their peace, wisdom, and love is the years have taught them these truths about themselves, freeing them to humbly come to God. *The key isn't the destitution per se, but that destitution caused them to immerse themselves in God and discover his love.* The bravado of rightness, of prideful proving and protecting at the top or center, gave way to humble surrender at the bottom and the edges of things.

In what ways is this happening for you?

True coming to God makes possible for all of Christ's followers a dynamic correspondence that is foundational to living in his presence, and this amazing spiritual reality is the focus of the next chapter.

For Discussion

1. Use your own words to describe what it means to come to God. How much does "coming" characterize your own faith journey?

2. Why is coming continually to God in Christ the most significant thing we can do to find the reality of God?

3. Do you think religious performance might distract you from true coming? Explain.

4. What did you learn about "coming" from the story of the sinful woman? How is destitution a gift?

5. Explain how the imagery of a gatekeeper being attentive to someone approaching his gate and welcoming them inside captures the essence of Christian spirituality.

6. Give an example of how God blesses us through coming attitudes. Which attitudes challenged you, and why? Where do you think you are on the progressive sequence?

7. How can you order your life to give the Spirit a chance to form coming attitudes in you?

CHAPTER 5

A Dynamic Correspondence

But if you look carefully into the perfect law that sets
you free, and if you do what it says and don't forget
what you heard, then God will bless you for doing it.

—JAMES 1:25 (NLT)

The greatest blessing of coming to God is to truly encounter *him*.[64]
Think about what happens when you open your heart to someone
else. If their heart is also open to you, there is the possibility of a
dynamic "correspondence" between you, ongoing exchanges and
interaction—spending time together, conversation, and doing things
with or for the other. Correspondence in the rich sense of two people
relating or being *co-responsive*. Now imagine the other Person is God.
This *relational* rather than merely *utilitarian* view to encountering
God is much more hopeful, exciting, and biblically complete.

"Relating"

Concerning our relationship with God, we tend to zero in on
what we must do to qualify for love, rather than what relating
actually means. My son Reuben had to be resuscitated at birth and,
as with each of our children, before he took a breath our hearts
were bursting at the seams with love for him. We were related

by blood, yes, but the relationship wasn't real until I touched his spluttering little body, and he momentarily opened his eyes in acknowledgment. This dynamic correspondence—receiving something and then responding—is the kernel of relating. Importantly, it is non-negotiable if we are to relate authentically with God, because it realizes his presence, giving us ways to immerse our lives in him. It makes his omnipresence real for *us*.

Think for a minute about how to counter spiritual flatness. If a car won't start, we don't try to fit a jet-pack on the roof; we go back and check the basics. Do we have fuel? Is the battery dead? Are the spark plugs okay? *In the spiritual life, when inspiration is missing, we go back and check the basics.* James, the brother of Jesus offered a nuts-and-bolts way forward (see James 1:25): read what the Bible teaches and put it into practice.

To *relate* means to correspond with proper respect. With friends, this means having a mutual sense of love. Corresponding with God can mean nothing less than "hearing" his Word of love—meaning we both receive or come to know his love and understand what God wants us to do—and responding with expressions of love and acts of obedience.

Be careful you don't assume a relationship with God by the fact of the blood of Christ—a legal relationship—without actually corresponding with him.[65] What, then, is the purpose of Christ's blood? The apostle Paul thought being reconciled to God meant something closer to a correspondence: "And since, when we were his enemies, we were brought back to God by the death of his Son, what blessings he must have for us now that we are his friends, and he is living within us!" (Rom. 5:10 TLB). How real is your own correspondence with God?

The Basic Paradigm: Corresponding in the Garden

The centrality of a dynamic correspondence for life with God hits you in the face in the Garden of Eden. The very fact God spoke to Adam and Eve in the garden (see Gen. 1:26–28) was no small thing—it signaled his patronage of the human creature. He exercised a divine paternal instinct by offering them the opportunity to live a life shaped by every word from the mouth of God (Matt. 4:4)—a higher-order life beyond the dust-to-dust rhythms of creaturely existence.

> Even before he made the world, God loved us and chose us in Christ to be holy and without fault in his eyes. God decided in advance to adopt us into his own family by bringing us to himself through Jesus Christ. This is what he wanted to do, and it gave him great pleasure (Eph. 1:4–5 NLT).

The mythical gods of the Greeks and Babylonians were not patrons at all. They left humanity in the meaningless cycles of creaturely life by remaining silent, *but Yahweh spoke to us*. It was a powerful prophetic act anticipating our ability to hear and respond in ways that would both draw us to a higher existence and glorify him. God stacked the deck by making humans response-*able*. Helmut Thielicke, the German theologian, said that to be human and made in the image of God is to have the capacity to hear and obey God's Word instead of our own rights and desires.

Before God's image in humans was mangled by the Fall, it was natural for Adam and Eve to correspond dynamically with God and, consequently, Eden was paradise. Hearing and obeying made God's Word personally transformational rather than just truth echoing through the cosmos. *They coexisted with God in the Garden, showing that hearing and obeying God is a basic paradigm for what it means to live in his presence.*[66] As soon as they put a halt to hearing and responding, they were bundled out of the garden and God's presence.

In a culture preoccupied with acquisition and ownership, it doesn't come naturally to hold things loosely and wait on the answer to the question, "What are you saying, Father?" In our post-Fall world, the image of God remains in us, but our response-*ability* has been impaired. It must now be regenerated by the Holy Spirit so God's Word ignites our hearts with extravagant delight for him, and we eagerly obey like children do before they lose their innocence.

The Voices of a Fallen World

Being unwilling to hear and respond to God has a cost: we forfeit his patronage and presence, and our life will inevitably be shaped by the voice of the devil or self. These voices of the Fall drag us down and away from God's reality or presence.

> Separation from the Presence is, quite literally, what the Fall *is*. As a result of the Fall, mankind slipped from God-consciousness into the hell of self and self-consciousness. Such a state is at once sinful and incomplete. This fallen self, turned inward and narcissistic, dwells in misconceived feelings and attitudes, those that arise from listening to the self-in-separation and to the voices of a fallen world.[67]

As a simple example, God's voice affirms we are valuable and dearly loved by him. Embracing this truth edifies and empowers our souls—it is the by-product of a dynamic correspondence and living in God's presence. But by rejecting God's voice, we subject ourselves to other voices telling us we don't amount to much. Our souls are burdened as a natural consequence of failing to correspond. Consider your own similar experiences.

Adam and Eve could not disobey and stay in God's presence. They died spiritually by ignoring God's Word—with no correspondence or patronage. God might as well have been a mythical deity to them, as he is for many Christians today who worship dutifully in a flatland. *A warning bell rings here against slipping into spiritual death because we assume a relationship with God when we are not actually corresponding at all!* Like the frog in the pot of water being heated slowly to boiling, good Christians can slip from God consciousness without realizing what's happening, until they die.

Is your real correspondence with God consistent with what you assume it to be?

Josh and Amy's Story

Josh broke up with the girl he loved because, in his words, he "wanted to be a spiritual somebody and really please God." He moved into a house full of friends determined to live and love as Jesus did. But Josh could sense the basis for his passion was about pleasing God rather than relating to him, and this was limiting his experience of God.

He started doing solitary retreats in the Blue Mountains National Park. Was this spiritual bravado? Was Josh driven by hunger for more? Whatever else it may have been, this was a setup. As Josh gave God a chance to speak, he did! Josh discovered God loved him—in his words, "the Creator of the universe looked at me with genuine affection!" He recounts sitting in a cave with recognition that the love of God was more real than the tree in front of him.

Josh married his girlfriend, Amy, and in the challenges and busyness of a young family they are trying to prioritize time to simply be with God, hear his love, and respond naturally with trust and obedience rather than just trying to please God.

"Remain in Me"

Jesus didn't mince words: unless his disciples correspond with him, they should not presume life with God would be on tap or that their lives would bear fruit and please God.

You are already clean because of the word I have spoken to you. Remain in me, as I also remain in you. No branch can bear fruit by itself; it must remain in the vine. Neither can you bear fruit unless you remain in me (John 15:3–4).

He unveils the single priority for a follower of Christ: *to remain in him*. This is inner-circle insight, essence. It cuts to the chase. Delving into what Jesus meant, we will see he is, in fact, calling his disciples into a synthesis of our paradox.

Using the Greek word *meno* for "remain," Jesus is saying, "Be at home and at rest in me, and let my love, teaching, priorities, habits, and call settle and be at home in you." (my paraphrase) We can be physically present with someone but distant. Our thoughts, affections, priorities, and interests dwell elsewhere. No intimacy exists. Jesus is saying, "Correspond with me in a manner allowing the sap of my life to flow into you and to form the life of love there." (my paraphrase). *God is thrilled to dwell in the sort of life that makes room for him.* But without the vital connection of "remaining" that facilitates this we are fruitless deadwood living outside the sphere of love.

Hearing the God Who Speaks

Others have written excellent books specifically addressing hearing God. For example, *4 Keys to Hearing God's Voice* by Mark and Patti Virkler provides a simple and powerful approach based on the following four keys:[68]

1. *Spontaneity*: Recognize God's voice as spontaneous thoughts that light upon your mind.
2. *Stillness*: Quiet yourself so you can hear God's voice.
3. *Vision*: Look for vision as you pray.
4. *Journaling*: Write down the flow of thoughts and pictures that light upon your mind.

Ruth Haley Barton in *Pursuing God's Will Together: A Discernment Practice for Leadership Groups* helps a leadership group make the game-changing shift from decision-making based on worldly wisdom, to discernment—"seeing" what God is doing and what he desires as the basis for our attitudes and action.[69] Suggestions in chapter 9 for positioning ourselves for the Holy Spirit to instruct our hearts will also be helpful.

The Bible teaches that God speaks to us through his providence (see Acts 14:17), our consciences (see Rom. 2:14–15), his Son (see Heb.1:2), and creation (see Ps. 19:1–2, Rom. 1:20). In the Old and New Testaments, God spoke through dreams, visions, inner impressions, prophecies, words of knowledge, and in other supernatural ways, and this continued even after Jesus ascended to the Father. For example, Philip's experience with the Ethiopian eunuch in Acts 8 includes an angelic visitation and the Holy Spirit speaking directly to him. Seeing the Bible as the *only* source of revelation today may be "safe" but it is also unbiblical. Scripture clearly teaches we should expect God to communicate with us in a variety of ways. Jesus encouraged his followers to expect God to speak directly to them by the Holy Spirit. (See also Luke 12:11–12 and 21:14–15). In the New Testament, God's will was also discerned as a community decision-making process involving the asking of questions and listening to the views of others.

This opens us to the biblical reality that God is always speaking to us within our own hearts and we can learn to discern his voice. Mark and Patti Virkler make the point that many of the thoughts in our minds are not *our* thoughts, and the flow of spontaneous thoughts coming across the inner screen of our minds and hearts is coming from the spirit world.[70] Our own thoughts are analytical, but what God projects onto our inner screen is sensed as *spontaneous* thoughts that light upon our mind. They can come in a specific situation or as we meditate on Scripture. They facilitate the powerful ministry of the Holy Spirit through us but should not be sought solely for this purpose, but as God's healing, empowering, and guiding voice into every aspect of our lives.

Trusting that there is a constant flow of communication from God flowing through each of us all the time is foundational for hearing him—we must believe that he exists and will respond with goodness when we seek him. Can you embrace this truth?

Walter, who is part of our church community, said that hearing God speak took a long time for him because of what was in the way—the thinking and attitudes formed by his religious but not so spiritual upbringing. He says, "As I peel back the layers, move myths out, renounce false beliefs . . . the more I relax and seek to hear the voice of Jesus, the more I hear. Slowly, slowly, the more I lean in, the more he speaks and lives."

The fundamental challenge in hearing God's voice does not lie in coaxing God to speak but in being quiet enough and pure in heart enough to discern his voice above the voices of our fallen world. Each voice has a distinctive tone. *The devil's voice is demeaning.* It will accuse and condemn us, leaving a residue of guilt and shame in our souls, or goad us to perform to earn love. *Our own voice is self-absorbed.* This voice will puff us up and promise success to feed our search for significance. But *God's voice affirms the sacred value of our lives as his loved children* whatever our performance and graciously summon us to follow Christ's way of love in service of God's kingdom.

Hannah Whitall Smith tested impressions from the Holy Spirit by whether they were in harmony with Scripture, seemed up to scratch to her Spirit-enlightened common sense, and also whether, as Quakers say, a "way opens" for them to be carried out.[71] Ignatius of Loyola gauged his inward experience after making a choice to test the spirits or discern whether his choice was from God—*consolation* (inner peace, freedom, a sense of life and connection with God) was evidence that he had heard from God while *desolation* (inner turmoil, a sense of being out of touch with God and others) showed he had not.[72] God can also speak powerfully to us as we listen carefully to others.

Through heart-work (see Rom. 12:1–2) the spiritual muddle that prevails when all the voices have an equal say is replaced by spiritual clarity and sharpness. We should pray for indifference toward anything except God's will before asking God to speak.[73] Otherwise it is like trying to hear with an idol in our hearts— an agenda, issue, or something we hanker after—filtering and distorting the answer.[74] *If we are ready to obey what God says, we will have a better time of hearing him.* We will hear God more accurately through Scripture if we read it more deeply as Jesus did—through the lens of his Father's love (see Lk. 6:6–11).

Do you desire to hear God speak? If so, how could you work on hearing him better?

The Beauty and Power of Obedience

There's no other way to be happy in Jesus but to trust and obey, as the old hymn says. Obedience is integral to the natural rhythm of corresponding with God, but its spiritual value is hard to see until we can hear God's *love* ringing out from the first and the greatest commandments:

> I am the LORD your God. . . . You shall have no other gods before me (Ex. 20:2–3).

> Love the Lord your God with all your heart and with all your soul and with all your strength and with all your mind (Lk. 10:27).

These calls for no-compromise respect express love because when we hear *and* obey God's Word it sculpts our lives into sacred designs expressing his love. The lives of mockers or mere hearers, however, are inevitably shaped by the voices of this fallen world.

In the same way, by becoming man, being crucified and gloriously resurrected, Jesus demonstrates his lordship. This commands the sort of respect that won't tolerate our being careless hearers, but rather disciples who do his will. *This is significant because it is in obedient response to his lordship, as we follow him, that we find God's transforming grace and light* (John 8:12).

Obedience gets us on the dancefloor with the God who restores.

Today we are more likely to say, "Nobody feels called or has the time to witness, pray for the sick, or feed the poor, so God obviously doesn't want to do these things now!" We make God's will variable and dodge obedience but forfeit a transforming dance with God.

Let's be frank for a moment. When God's wonderful kindness in Christ hit us and we offered our lives to him, what did we think this would mean? Anything less than obedience—trading our will for God's—places us outside of dynamic correspondence with God. We are always unlike God to some degree, so how will we move toward oneness with God (John 17:21) if we are not being changed? Sidestepping obedience limits our experience of his love!

The issue isn't moral perfection, but ongoing responsiveness in terms of what matters to God.[75] Salvation is not a matter of yes or no, in or out, but an ongoing and real liberation, transformation, and union with God as we immerse ourselves in him. Similarly, God's kingdom is both now and not yet. Because it is both here (God is at work) and still coming (God has more to do), we aren't just statically in or out of the kingdom but dynamically encountering more of it as we expectantly interact with God. Consider for a moment what you are after in God: Is it yes-no or dynamic encounter?

When we are caught up in a dynamic correspondence with God that is catalyzed and fueled by love, how can this do anything but delight our souls? Inward peace, for example, is a blessing one receives through obedience to God's commandments (see Isa. 48:18). Our obedience delights God's heart (John 14:23), but why? Is it because his loved children get involved with him (when my children do this my heart bursts)? Does he feel honored? Is it joy from seeing our lives improve? Or perhaps the ways in which our obedience serves his efforts in the cosmic battle against darkness? Such is the deep mystery of the beauty and power of obedience in the spiritual realm.

It is crystal clear, though, that our response to God is not our ultimate goal. God is. God is the source of love and the goal of love.

The Grace Escape

Despite all this, we often seem bent on convincing ourselves that because we are under the umbrella of grace, it is not imperative to find out what God asks us to do and then actually *do* it. For example, the takeaway from Martha and Mary's story (see Lk. 10:38–42) often is this: sitting at the feet of Jesus to listen to his words is exemplary and doing things for him is twisted. But this is missing the point. Doing things for God *for any reason other than as a response to hearing his Word of love* is spiritually unhealthy. We must *hear* God's Word *and do it* if we want to correspond dynamically with him. Luke peppers his readers with this message in the lead-up to the visit to Mary and Martha's house (see Lk. 8:4-15, 21; 10:25-37). Jesus did not see any legalism in obeying his teaching *if we love him* (John 14:23). Legalism looms only if we are *qualifying* for God's love rather than *responding* to it. No forcing from our Master. We must choose to obey out of oneness of spirit. As friends of the Bridegroom, we find that responding obediently to his voice might offer challenges, but it is not a tussle of wills and brings us great joy (see John 3:29–30). Thomas à Kempis could write, "O sweet and delightful service of God by which a person is made truly free and holy!"[76]

Ironically, escaping obedience under the grace-umbrella impacts us at the final judgment. We will not be punished, condemned, or stripped of our salvation for shoddy performance (see John 5:24). Instead, believers will be judged as the basis for bestowing levels of *reward* (see Rev. 22:12).

So, let's say a passionate "Yes!" to responding to God's Word. Let's resolve to stand out as followers of Jesus because our lives look, smell, and act like his—clear as day! When inward conviction hits us, let's welcome the guidance of the Spirit and cooperate to make some God-glorifying changes in our lives. When we have a tender conscience, even about little things, we place ourselves smack-dab in the middle of a dynamic correspondence with God.

Corresponding has Cosmic Significance

Before the Fall, Eden was paradise because man's will was one with God's. It was natural for created beings to correspond with God, to be ready to hear and obey his voice. God's love and wisdom defined their existence. They honored God.

The devil's spoiler strategy was to have Adam and Eve pridefully stop corresponding with God. *The heart or will became the focus of this battle precisely because this is where the attitudes are formed that free a person to correspond with God.* When we are freed to do the will of God from the heart (see Eph. 6:6), the angels and demons know God's grace has prevailed (see Eph. 3:10). Christ's work on the Cross also speaks about the cosmic importance of corresponding:

> The deepest meaning of the cross is to give up "one's own I." Only when this dark tyrant has been wounded unto death can undisturbed peace rule. . . . [W]e seek no longer to maintain our own authority; we gladly lay the government upon His shoulder who is called the Prince of Peace (Isaiah 9:6). . . . [A]s far as his government extends, so far extends also our peace.[77]

The devil urged Adam and Eve to exalt their "I," trading God's will for their own and forfeiting God's creative influence. Evil, suffering, and pain infiltrated the creation on the back of this second will (and every subsequent will). The Devil's *coup d'état* birthed the proud idea in the heart of created beings that they have the capacity to find peace without God. The devil tempted Eve to define life for herself, and billions of wills entered the creation.[78] It's worth noting here the temptation of Adam and Eve involved *rejecting* obedience. The creation stopped corresponding, and without God's Word calling out, defining, and sustaining a life of love, human life became small and needy. Adam and Eve's fear and shame were the first fruits of this life of their own making. As Oscar Wilde said, "When the gods wish to punish us, they answer our prayers."

God's redemptive plan to display his glory centers on restoring creation to its pre-Fall state (see Rev. 21:1–4) with only one will: God's (see Matt. 6:10). By dealing with sin, the goal is to restore every human being to the dynamic corresponding with God that made Eden paradise.

The Will and Sin

As Dallas Willard wrote: "From [the will] the whole self is directed and organized. . . . That is why we recognize the will to be the same as the biblical heart or center."[79] It is difficult to neatly separate the heart, soul, mind, and spirit when discussing the non-physical part of a person. What we feel and think influences our choices—the exercise of our will. In turn, we can choose what we allow ourselves to feel and what concepts and images we entertain in our minds. Scripturally, the mind is not confined to physical and intellectual perception, but includes the power to arrive at moral judgments.

Since the heart is the center and source of the physical life and the inner life, with its thinking, feeling, and volition, unless the will is surrendered to God, the heart is not. The will is the God-given freedom and creativity to make choices that determine the expression of a human life in the world, and organizes a human life around God. *Our spiritual life must therefore impact us deeply enough to touch the will.*

The exercise of our will forms character as choices become ingrained. In this sense, the heart or will is who we are and determines who we will become. It is the operating system of the self—good or bad. It is what is true about us. Importantly, it is what God knows and looks at when he corresponds with us.

Sin is a personal deviation from God's will, and the theological fact that even God's loved children struggle with sin (i.e., not a moralistic judgment about whether people are good or bad) says that "humans are not close to God, and are not serving God."[80] This means the possibility of a dynamic correspondence with God is not just a matter of some surface tinkering with our resolve. No way! *Sin smashes the possibility of life with God because it drags our will away from his, and it can only be restored by recognizing our sin and—as God's loved children—receiving God's generous forgiveness.* Under such grace, the core of our being, our will, surrenders.

Cunning Counterfeits

We can see the genuine more clearly by looking at a counterfeit. Given the spiritual importance of corresponding with God, it shouldn't surprise us that cunning counterfeits abound—all that is needed is a slight warping of the way we think (see 2 Cor. 10:4–5). Following is a summary of five counterfeit ways of corresponding with God that sharpen our understanding of what God is after.

Counterfeit 1: **BELIEFISM**[81] is about believing the words of Jesus but without any corresponding belief-fueled action. We lap up a sermon series on "Loving One Another" but don't change the way we treat others. Demons recognize Jesus but won't come under his authority (see James 2:19). This counterfeit stands on an unbiblical idea: that simply agreeing that Christ's words are true (supported by our mantra of Jesus-talk such as saying "in the name of Jesus," and surrounding ourselves with Christian schools and bumper stickers) is the sum of faith. Our sole responsibility is to arbitrate on the rightness of God's Word like pew-bound magistrates, to hash out what is true in our Bible studies, because for us, salvation is about nailing down what is right rather than doing what Jesus says. For example, embracing the *point* of the "Parable of the Good Samaritan" is enough, we think, to consider ourselves "willing," whether or not we ever help people in need. All of Christ's basic commands are demoted in the same way. *So we have lots of opinions about right doctrine but not many personal stories about involving dynamically with God.*

Is this true in your life? What would you give for some stories of your own?

Jesus clearly taught that beliefism leaves us like the man who built his life on sand, and that we should put his words into practice if we want a strong and good life (see Matt. 7:24–27).

Counterfeit 2: VIRTUAL FOLLOWING *simulates* true following through passion about interesting issues, doctrinal debates, music, the supernatural, and the like, while actually being bored with Jesus and what is central to him.

Jake seemed passionate about Jesus, went to any meeting promising the supernatural, and lapped up fresh teaching, but his eyes glazed over at the prospect of being still to listen to God or reading the Bible. I invited him to help out serving poor families. Jake didn't have time. He was a "virtual follower."

Jake was looking for something deeper to fill the gap between his expectation of a radical Christianity and his own experience, but like many bored believers, he tried latching onto marginal issues and activities that barely registered in Christ's teaching. *This trapped him as a virtual follower, bored with the teaching of Jesus, because it's proved radical only in the doing.*

Counterfeit 3: COMMITMENT WITHOUT CONVICTION. The deception that performing measured Christian actions is the same as wholehearted love for God and neighbor is commitment without conviction.

John Wesley taught that being a good person by living out the rules of the day (i.e., being honest, not stealing, donating clothes or money superfluous to our real needs to a good cause) makes you an "almost Christian."[82] If you do nothing Christ's gospel forbids, live by the Golden Rule, maintain peace, do good deeds, take worship seriously, have family prayers, participate in the means of grace (such as communion), even sincerely desire to please God, if for a religious motivation such as avoiding punishment, you are just an "almost Christian," because you have *no better principle in the heart.*[83] For Wesley, discovery of God's love would so engage genuine Christians inwardly that they would love God extravagantly and be generously proactive for the good of others. Measured Christian actions are counterfeit.

Yes, Western life is complex and makes the way of Jesus a daunting challenge, but if it matters we can seek help and invest in our spiritual growth. Right? But many don't. Forget perfection; willingness is our intentional, consistent, honest, bumbling, best attempt to obey our Master, wanting to want him because of even a grain of conviction about him and his love.

What do the practices of your everyday life tell you about your conviction?

Counterfeit 4: CAFETERIA-STYLE FAITH.

It is tempting to selectively interpret the Scriptures to serve ourselves. For example, Nehemiah was incensed when fellow Jews charged excessively high interest rates to struggling farmers who had extended themselves in service to Jerusalem (see Neh. 5). The lending of money was not wrong in itself,[84] but according to Jewish law it was wrong to seek profit from someone else's hardship. They emphasized the law permitting them to charge interest and ignored the laws about not profiting from the calamity of others. They treated God's law like a cafeteria line where you could take what suits your taste and reject what doesn't. *What is permissible crowds out the deeper responsibility to please God by expressing love.*

Another example is the Corinthians' embracing Paul's teaching on grace with regard to Jewish laws about eating food sacrificed to idols, observing special days, and circumcision (see Rom. 14:14–15), but failing to consider how others less liberated might follow suit and be plagued by guilt for doing so. His point: not all that is "permissible is beneficial" (1 Cor. 10:23–24): doing something right doesn't allow us to ignore the broader scope of God's Word and heart of love as if choosing dishes to add to our tray to indulge our taste.

The genius of the counterfeit is that it uses God's Word to do violence to the rhythm of love that is its very heart, thereby crippling true correspondence with God. It deceives us into believing we ourselves get to determine the emphasis, priority, and urgency of the different aspects of God's Word and way of love. We arbitrate whether it means *me* or *now* and *how much*.

Can you identify ways you fall into this trap?

Counterfeit 5: IDOLATROUS DEVOTION.

When we let God define the shape and meaning of our lives, our correspondence with him is called *devotion*. The counterfeit: saying we are devoted to Christ but then whittling God down to the sort of god that fits our lifestyle.

In the first century, rabbis didn't recruit disciples, they chose a respected teacher and tried to gain admittance into his circle to learn.[85] God has chosen us (Eph. 1:3-14) but we must also choose Christ in the same way first-century disciples willingly submitted to the authority, influence, interests, and habits of their chosen rabbi.

The ex-leper's return to Jesus (see Lk. 17:15–16) is seen as an example of true devotion. Prostrate at the feet of Jesus he is joyfully and gratefully under orders saying, "I respect, trust, and submit to your authority over my life as my king and leader. I'm ready to be part of whatever is next on your agenda. To hear you is to respond." Do you think Christ truly defines the shape of your life, and why?

If, however, *we* are defining God, this is called *idolatry*—simply forming our own concept or idea of God, and bowing down to it. Some cultures carve idols from wood. In the West, we seem adept at making idols out of anything and everything—sports, career, physical appearance, sex, music, money, houses, cars, celebrities, and academic knowledge. Whether we carve a wooden idol or find something other than God that is self-gratifying to which we give the defining rights over our lives, the result is the same—we will end up spiritually deaf, blind, and lifeless because we are not corresponding with a life-giving God (see Ps. 135:15–18).

We may say we are devoted to Christ but then whittle God down to the sort of god that fits our lifestyle and serves our own will—one that gives us rights to our time, spiritualizes an unbalanced focus on wealth creation, exempts us from helping the poor so we can serve ourselves, or defines worship in terms of a few songs on Sunday. This is clearly not the same as being gloriously defined by God as we hear his Word and respond. What sort of God do you worship?

These counterfeits linger enticingly just degrees from the real thing to snag sleepy believers, so it pays to understand them. I encourage you to reflect honestly on your own correspondence with God to hone and sharpen it.

Is It Really True?

This chapter leads us to say the following: if the Bible is true, then we can correspond dynamically with God. People living in subsistence cultures live day by day with expectation that food will come from somewhere—a catch of fish, garden vegetables; they believe in that story. The danger of living so long after Christ's coming is we live as if God here and now is only a *theoretical* possibility. Rather than plunge into a dynamic correspondence with God, instead we perpetually search for supporting evidence.

Do you think God here and now is a *real* or *theoretical* possibility?

By corresponding dynamically with God we step into God's life-flow and our unique, God-planned, and most-alive existence. The next chapter develops a model for discipleship integrating our discussion about the spiritual life, the specific practice of corresponding with God, and the discovery of this sacred and powerful life.

For Discussion

1. Do you relate to God in terms of what we must do to qualify for love or in terms of what it actually means to "relate"? Explain.

2. In the Bible, what are the elements of the basic paradigm for corresponding with God? How does Adam and Eve's experience apply to us today?

3. Discuss the issues you face in hearing God speak. What "voices of the fallen world" influence your life? What does *God* say about these areas or issues in your life, and how does that change things?

4. Does the call to obedience liberate you or oppress you? Explain why.

5. Which of the counterfeits apply to your life, and how will you address them?

6. Why is our will important for corresponding with God, and how does this make the spiritual life important?

CHAPTER 6

An Integrated Model for Discipleship

Is the life I am living the same as the
life that wants to live in me?

—PARKER J. PALMER

So far, we have focused on a model for discipleship that helps us to understand something important: *spirituality* is integral to following Jesus. If our goal is to live close to the Creator, then we need to cultivate a spiritual life with the firepower to bring about the following:

- a lasting discovery of God's love;
- authentic soul-transformation;
- "barefoot" attitudes conducive to a dynamic correspondence with God; and
- shifts in our will freeing us to move against the grain and toward love.

How does your spiritual life stack up to this? Anything less, which allows us to "do Christian things" on the surface, will forever fall short. *If any model for discipleship is to be fruitful, we must seriously integrate spirituality into it.*

What Must Discipleship Achieve?

There are five important transitions that highlight what we should expect from true biblical discipleship.

1. FROM ENGINEERING CHURCH LIFE TO RELEASING ITS SACRED LIFE

Equipping churchgoers for church jobs to make them feel useful and to make the church "work" shrinks discipleship down to making members feel good. The goal, stripped of divine imagination and scope, diminishes. Tasks such as inviting people, ministering on a prayer team, welcoming visitors, and leading a small group to assimilate newcomers, are worth doing. But the sense of discipleship in the New Testament just isn't in the ballpark of engineering church life. It arcs into another spiritual dimension altogether with the idea of *releasing* the sacred life of the Church—the liberating discovery of God and his love, passionate love for him, and realizing the unique flow of God's love out from each of us to bless our world.

We *reproduce* the life of Christ; the seed of this life is awakened and grows in us as we consistently allow opportunity for inward watering by the Holy Spirit and encounters of the loving presence of Christ. It is evidenced by the fruit of the Spirit (see Gal. 5:22–23) and the works of the kingdom. And with the release of Christ's life in us *reproduction* happens on another level as well—we make disciples of others who also reproduce the life of Christ (Matt. 28:18–20).

Writing on finding one's true calling, Parker Palmer asks, "Is the life I am living the same as the life that wants to live in me?"[86] How would you answer this question?

The life that presses within us for expression is our sacred and true life, our flying life, which God wove into our DNA to reflect his image. We can't find it without God because his love is too foreign to be naturally on our radar; we only know what to look for when we see it in him. Pastor and social activist Gordon

Cosby understood that knowing who we are—deeply loved children of God who bear his image for the purpose of expressing it in the world—helps us know what we are to do with God, and to believe that God will do it through us. Once we grasp what we are intended to be, we can ask, "What is the appropriate doing for that being?" If God's own being is built into us, at some point we must make choices allowing it to find expression.[87]

We are wired for our sacred life. But *sin and our sacred life don't mix because the first expresses our will while the latter finds its shape in God's.* The key New Testament words for "disciple" stem from *manthano*, meaning to learn by acquiring customs and habits through experience or practice. Far beyond merely gaining the skills or instruction needed for doing something, this sort of learning re-forms us inwardly. Jesus taught that we live from the inside out (see Matt.15:19), meaning inward change signals the birthing of a fresh way of being and therefore of behaving. *When we consistently acquire Christ's customs or habits through practice, experience, and inward reformation, our sacred life is released.*

Our souls experience our sacred and true life when we experience God's acceptance or do something truly noble, pure, generous, creative, loving, life-giving, or free. For example, think of the euphoria we experience when doing something purely for someone else, or our sense of well-being when we are free of fear and can follow our hearts. *Not surprisingly, our sacred lives uniquely reflect the life of love both in the receiving and the giving.*

Out on faith's edge, love frees us to dance in the rays of God and express his love here, there, and everywhere. We relinquish control to abandon ourselves to the sacred "not yet" of God, like the creative possibilities for which an artist reaches. We pray with authority to restore the sick. Our hands, homes, finances, and friendships serve the poor. Our existence finds its stride in what is life-giving about the Creator—things beyond our ego. Transcending its own predictable flatland, our soul feels the textures of being fully alive in love. We rediscover adventure, surprise, delight, God, worship, his power, and other people! It is the beautiful life of Christ, the sacred life of love. *When a critical mass within a church community has its sacred life released, its corporate life finds spiritual wings.*

God's mercy grabs us and angles us toward what pleases him (see 2 Cor. 5:9) so he can make us beautiful, strong, and durable, like oak trees to display his glory (see Isa. 61:3b). In the words of Saint Irenaeus: "Man fully alive is the glory of God." Both coming fully alive and living for the glory of God are part of our bigger, sacred lives. When our lives glorify God, we hit our "sweet spot" because we live authentically; the life for which divine hands created us.

Discipleship should liberate and prepare the followers of Jesus to be in the thick of bringing the kingdom to bless our world and restore God's creation. Jesus intended his followers to receive authority from him so they could exercise the power and love of God to liberate and restore people's lives (Lk. 9:1), but he returned from his transfiguration to find some of his disciples unable to free a boy tormented by an evil spirit (see Lk. 9:37–43). Frustrated, he modeled the sacred life by rebuking the evil spirit and healing the boy.

His frustration stemmed from the disciples' failure to take kingdom initiative and responsibility in faith—a recurrent issue as Jesus tried to pass the kingdom ministry baton to his disciples.[88] They crowded in under the umbrella of Christ's initiative but didn't *originate* actions aimed at healing the sick, serving the poor, or witnessing to those still searching for God. The dilemma: who would take responsibility or follow through *on core kingdom business* after Jesus ascended to heaven? Our calling is to take initiative and responsibility as instruments of God's spiritual authority, power, and love in such a way that we can say, "The kingdom of God is near you right now!"

Do you feel your life in Christ has been "engineered" or "released"? Why?

2. FROM "VICARIOUS CHRISTIANITY"
TO FIRSTHAND INVOLVEMENT WITH GOD

"Vicarious Christianity" describes a life of faith lived through others or through the machinery of the church organization—involvement with God through the faith, prayers, insights, and ministry exploits of others. The preacher, for example, tells us what God is saying. When the church machine reaches out to help the needy, we reach out too, despite the fact we don't actually do anything! Can you identify some ways your involvement with God is secondhand? Real involvement with God might not be what we expected or it may include suffering, but it will bring joy in time (see John 15:10–11).[89] Different from pleasure, the joy Jesus promises "arises from the sense of a finished work. It is a creative joy, like the joy of an artist."[90] We are in the zone of our intended existence—hearts in play and our lives immersed in Jesus. Discipleship should lead us there.

We also forfeit true relationship with God if the sum of our involvement is our intellectual ideas about God. We beaver away at crafting better expressions of truth and offer them to God as if he is lacking in true ideas about himself. But he *is* Truth. What we can give God that he otherwise doesn't have is *our response* to truth. Otherwise, listening to sermons and doing Bible studies won't lead to the dynamic involvement with God discipleship should achieve. This doesn't devalue preaching or Bible study, but rather sharpens their worth.

In the same way, we offer musically better worship songs as if God is musically deprived, but he is the very Rhythm, Melody, and Lyric of the cosmos. What we can give God he otherwise doesn't have is the song from *our* hearts. Better musicianship does not constitute a truer involvement with God.

Soul-level involvement forms a highway bringing salvation (see Ps. 50:8–23). It is the X factor in our transformation because the Spirit has access to the parts of us needing to be loved, healed, reformed, and empowered.

In the Gospels, a range of people discovered the sacred sweetness and power of their lives through firsthand involvement with Christ.[91] The Word of God incarnate in him summoned their sacred lives into being, and the Father's love in him freed them to it. How might the people clustered around Jesus in the Gospels provide a vision for your own spiritual life? Many became passionate worshipers and powerful witnesses with firsthand stories to tell of God's goodness. *This is what discipleship should achieve.*

3. FROM TOURISM TO PILGRIMAGE

The Hebrews went on pilgrimage up to the temple in Jerusalem singing the Songs of Ascents (see Ps. 120—134). As they sang, they were drawn into a dynamic correspondence with God, fueling their souls with hope, courage, wisdom, joy, and vision for the long journey up to the presence of God, represented by the temple. The title of Eugene Petersen's book *A Long Obedience in the Same Direction* describes it well.[92] Three times a year, they trekked up to Jerusalem for worship festivals (see Ex. 23:14–17), reenacting this metaphor of a life spent on a journey toward God. It is the pilgrim's journey of ten thousand steps Godward, the grace to correspond ceaselessly whether we are soaring on the heights or weeping in the valley—and whether we like it or not. *This is what discipleship should achieve.*

The challenge: Western culture espouses the dangerous idea we can reach our goals and procure what we want quickly and without raising a sweat. It's dangerous precisely because, biblically, life with God is more like the committed trek of the Hebrew pilgrims winding their way up to the temple. *Relationships by their nature are journeys.* They are dynamic, not static—more like the surging sea than an agreement on paper. When you go to the shops, you arrive there; with relationships, you reach higher levels but will always be traveling further. There is always more of God.

The comparison between *tourists* and *pilgrims* emphasizes the task of discipleship. Tourists live out their faith via the spiritual highlights. The rush, impatience for results, search for shortcuts, shortage of time, and an appetite for the latest and greatest—these are the attitudes that define Western life and shape its religion. Tourists consume packaged religious experiences at attractive sacred sites with pastors or conference speakers as tour guides, but don't venture into kingdom culture. It takes too much sweat and too much time. This attitude is similar to that of a businessman I met in Port Moresby. He stayed at the five-star Airways Hotel close to the airport because it was "for people who don't really want to come here." I had just been roughing it in a coastal village, catching coral trout and eating local food. *Tourists come to a place but haven't really traveled anywhere.* Spiritual tourism doesn't really lead to God.

Pilgrims are on a no-compromise barefoot journey, edging them steadily toward God by hearing and responding obediently for the long haul. Pilgrims grasp the nature of this journey and make time for it.

Tourists hankering for the next spiritual highlight reveal their immaturity by saying, "Are we there yet?" But pilgrims perceive they are already "there," on the journey of corresponding dynamically with God out where the leading edge of grace unfolds. *It is a journey we must contend for vigorously because of the tug of quick-fix Western ideas, but when we do, we keep our souls spiritually lean, fit, and hungry.*

This reminds me of racing small sailing boats as a kid. Finances were tight for our missionary family, and all we could fork out for was a rotting hull nobody else wanted. I patched it up with fiberglass, making it the heaviest boat in the class, and with Abrahamic faith emblazoned the name *Sonic* across the front. *Sonic* languished in last place until the prized North-West series. Winds of thirty knots lashed the fleet, forcing most crews to withdraw, and leaving *Sonic* trailing *Nicky-Noo*—the favorite and by far the best boat technically. Nearing the second-to-last turning buoy, *Nicky-Noo* lost its drain plug and began to sink, leaving *Sonic* to limp home for an unlikely win. On pilgrimage, we can feel as though everyone else is favored to win life's prize, but if we stay on the journey long enough, we position ourselves for God to act. I was toughened for the storm because every week I had to fight to be competitive. When we stick at the pilgrim's journey, our soul is lean and fit when the storms of life lash our lives. *Discipleship must bless us with the biblical perspective and spiritual fitness to position ourselves out on that edge of grace as pilgrims, and to hang on because spiritual highlights won't get us very far.*

Does tourism or pilgrimage best describe your own faith journey?

4. FROM PURPOSE TO PLAY

As we discussed in chapter 1, serving God's *purpose* is good, but something higher is *play*, or sharing in the joy and beauty of God. *Discipleship must not only have us serving God's purposes out of duty but doing so as a free and playful expression of our participation in the desires of the heart of God.* It must liberate us to be filled with joy like playful children when we do the loving and restoring things that bring God joy, express his beauty, and bless the world. Otherwise we will lack the spiritual vitality and spontaneity necessary to participate in the kingdom and fulfil the Great Commission. Besides, God is happy when his children find joy in "play."

Does your God-life feel like duty, or is it more free and playful?

5. FROM ONE DIMENSION TO MULTIPLE DIMENSIONS

There are dimensions to the life of Jesus that are not yet a natural part of our lives, and discipleship must help us attain them. Take the story recorded in Luke 9:51–56. On the way to Jerusalem the disciples are dispatched to a Samaritan village to line up lodgings but are not welcomed. James and John want to torch them with heavenly napalm. The disciples clutch onto the historic Jewish hostility toward the Samaritans like a dog with a bone and miss what God is doing, but Jesus is going to die for these same Samaritans—for him they are part of God's saving plan.[93]

"I work all week, and the weekend is for me." Rightly, this convention provides rest, but it also hampers our involvement in the kingdom as much as did the disciples' anti-Samaritan attitude. If we are consumed in our work during the week so we need to convalesce on the weekend, when will we serve Christ? There are many such conventions,[94] and Jesus is saying if we are bound by them, we will struggle to follow him wherever he goes; he will live in dimensions we don't. *Disciples aren't just spinning religious wheels but growing into the length, height, and depth of Christ's life by hearing his Word of love and responding.* Identify at least three ways you could grow into the dimensions of Christ's life.

To reinforce these five transitions we have just discussed, let's look at the way Jesus differentiated his own followers.

What Made the Disciples of Jesus Different

In Luke's Gospel, Jesus teaches his disciples "The Lord's Prayer" in response to their request, "Lord, teach us to pray, *just as John taught his disciples*" (Lk. 11:1b NLT, my emphasis). John's followers were known for certain practices that differentiated them from other sects in first-century Judaism,[95] and the disciples of Jesus are asking, "What is distinctive about *us*?"[96] Luke saw this prayer not just as words to parrot religiously but to engrave into the life of the community the dispositions, attitudes, and practices distinctive of the followers of Jesus.

> Father, may your name be kept holy. May your Kingdom come soon. Give us each day the food we need, and forgive us our sins, as we forgive those who sin against us. And don't let us yield to temptation (Lk. 11:2b–4 NLT).

First, as Christ's followers, we call God our Father. Others in the first century—both Jews and Gentiles—addressed God as "Father," but "tended to begin their prayers with titles stressing God's greatness [or] lordship."[97] This attitude of piety created a first impression of God as far away, above. But Jesus moved the recognition of God's greatness to *after* the invitation to intimacy. *As his followers we distinctively perceive God to be close and involved in our immediate lives because of his Father-love.* How do you see God?

We have shifted from outward piety as a means of trying to make God do something, to inward intimacy as a real connection with who God *already* is (loving, holy, powerful) and what he is *already* doing (bringing his kingdom). Guilty and ashamed we look into our Father's face and feel his transforming acceptance.

That God is *our* Father links us with others because they are his children too. First-century tradition was for sons to take on their father's business. In the same way, as God's children we take on his redemptive business to mercifully save and restore people in our Monday-to-Saturday lifestyle—not just those who can reciprocate or prop up our reputation, but the sort of people Jesus spent time with, such as the poor and powerless, outcasts, and those despised by society. Is this natural for you or is it a struggle? *Christ's followers are distinctively agents of change for a new brand of society with life-giving social interactions, because God is our Father.*[98]

Second, Christ's followers honor God's name. This means to make God and all he stands for (for example, love, justice, purity, power, restoration, and salvation) holy—the opposite of common. *We see special value in God and what he desires and reflect this in our attitude and actions.* People will do things in the name of a cause, a sports team, an ethnic group, decency, family, fairness, society's accepted values, success, patriotism, or being economically responsible. And we legitimize our lifestyle by honoring such names. But we are *Christ's* followers when we act on the basis of who God is and what he desires *above all other names.* Is this true of your life, or in practice do you honor other names more highly?

When we say we believe in God but ignore his wisdom or authority, and as a result act badly or struggle personally, we dishonor God (see Ezek. 36:16–24). *But we can fight for his honor by humbly asking God to go to work in us—to wash us, love us, change us, and call us to the love, purity, nobility, and purpose resonant in him.* Discipleship has its work cut out here.

Third, as the followers of Jesus, we believe the Good News— that with the coming of Jesus, the kingdom of God, his dynamic activity or rule, is breaking into the world. *God is here, at work in, around, and through our lives!* We are "live" with the seething reality of God's transforming love and resurrection power, his dreams for our lives, and all he feels, wills, and is doing infused through our daily existence. We jump in up to our ears in anticipation that Christ's coming initiated a decisive intervention by God into the world to defeat the powers that bring pain and death, and to progressively establish the new order of God's universal rule marked ultimately by "no more death or mourning or crying or pain" (Rev. 21:4). We seek to tune to the flow of God's life in and around us (see John 5:19) so that we can actively participate as instruments of divine mercy and blessing at church activities, while shopping, or barbecuing with friends. Do you feel that you are "live" with God?

Devoid of this perspective of the sheer privilege of kingdom involvement, we miss the point of Christian giving and wit-nessing. We scratch around with small-minded questions such as "Should we give gross or net?" and "money or time?" as if we are still trying to *qualify* for God's love. But the fundamental question related to giving is, "What do you want to do, God?" It's about *involving* with God because he has already stolen our hearts with gracious love (see 2 Cor. 8:5).

Does witness flow seamlessly from your faith, or is it a clunky, difficult add-on? Jesus told his disciples before Pentecost they would be filled with heavenly power by the Holy Spirit for the purpose of being his witnesses (see Acts 1:8). If we love someone it is natural to want to speak about them with others.

Fourth, as followers of Jesus, we are set apart by our reliance on God to provide the staples we need for our daily lives and our souls.[99] Think about what you really need to live: Acceptance? Healing? Peace? Provision? Jesus shows us how we should be toward God in the face of our needs and problems: *we ask like loved children, remain in a place of constant dependence through God-involvement, and get out of the kitchen and let him prepare the food.* Rather than push for what we want, we trust our Creator knows how to satisfy us better than anyone.

We ask for forgiveness and forgive others as a way of life in the Messianic community, because even God's loved children will struggle against sin and be sinned against. God will not fudge on sin because it hurts us, but he will generously forgive when we have the integrity in the middle of our failures and weakness to be sorry, ask for forgiveness, and reorient our lives toward what is right—a moment of pure grace or jubilee giving us a fresh start and release from guilt and shame. By repeated cycles of integrity, release, and reorientation, Christ's disciples find traction and momentum for their way toward Jesus.

Jesus makes it clear in his "Parable of the Unforgiving Servant" (see Matt. 18:21–35) that when we are generously forgiven but then mishandle this grace by failing to liberate others by forgiving them, we will forfeit our freedom and exchange it for captivity and punishment. A heart refusing to forgive cannot receive forgiveness itself. Hearing only the voices of this fallen world that focus on the injustice, pain, anger, fear, and guilt or shame of it, we can't hear God's healing voice of love. *Christ's followers pursue his presence to hear him speak words of truth: this disempowers the devil's lies and releases their hearts for freedom, joy, and love.*[100] Can you identify areas of your life that need healing and release?

Finally, fifth, Jesus differentiates his followers by a sober view of the journey. The kingdom is "now" *but also* "not yet." His followers embrace the reality that encountering evil and opposition is inevitable, that they will be left short of answers, lacking in faith and kingdom vision, with wrong desires fueling temptation, and needing God's help. They don't give up in the face of their weaknesses, difficulties, or the threat of temptation to draw them away from God's will, but through prayer they position themselves for assistance from heaven.[101]

Having explored what a discipleship model must achieve, we are now ready to build our model.

A Model for Discipleship Integrating Biblical Spirituality

We must go beyond seeing discipleship as a way to "operational effectiveness" for the church. We must instead address what it takes to change and become one with God, to discover and wade into our sacred life, and to develop the heart and spiritual skills to share in his coming reign.

STAGE 1: A FOUNDATIONAL PARADOX

In chapter 2, we established a foundational paradox governing life with God (see figure 1): on one hand, God's love for us has nothing to do with our performance (see Rom. 5:8); on the other hand, it is those who respond to God's Word who are blessed (see Lk. 11:27–28). So living with God requires we do both *nothing* to earn his love and *something* in response to it. As we recognized in chapter 5, hearing and responding to God constitutes the basic biblical paradigm for relating to God or living in his presence. It requires time for silence and solitude so that we can encounter his loving presence and hear his voice. It allows us to live in the sphere or economy of God's love—the space where God lives and works— as we receive love and express it to others. For all these reasons and because it characterized Christ's life, this dynamic correspondence with God forms the foundation for our discipleship model.

STAGE 2: THE "NORMAL CURVE"

The elements and dynamics of our model are represented by a normal curve.

A MODEL FOR DISCIPLESHIP

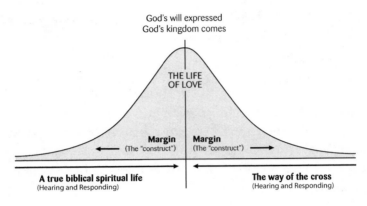

God's will expressed
God's kingdom comes

THE LIFE
OF LOVE

Margin
(The "construct")   ←

Margin
(The "construct")   →

A true biblical spiritual life
(Hearing and Responding)

The way of the cross
(Hearing and Responding)

FIGURE 3

Discipleship is a journey to the centerline of the curve, where life with God is richer and deeper. True discipleship always has God as the ultimate goal, and the church must not usurp him for anything.

The centerline stands for God's will or the expression of himself—genuine love. At the centerline we experience more of his kingdom coming (see Matt. 6:10). But, it also represents the economy of love we have been discussing, so as we move toward the centerline, the circle of our life overlaps more and more with the circle of God's life. We experience more of God and express more of his will and love, and in this sense, oneness or union with God.

The journey there requires we have enough insight into God's love to allow Jesus to have real authority over us. We are not called to make sacrifices to be extraordinary for God, but to take our ordinary lives and offer them entirely and wholeheartedly to him as our sacrifice. This means we accept the *nature* of divine author-ity, acknowledging both our worthiness to be loved by God as a gift and also our call to serve Christ's mission to bless the world.

Therefore the journey to the centerline will require higher levels of consciousness. We are transformed from being self-focused to realizing that others and their well-being are integral to our full existence. *To seek our own interests is to fall from love and live away from the centerline where life with God is most real.*

Richard Rohr describes four stained-glass windows in a Catholic church in India,[102] depicting the journey to higher levels of consciousness or spiritual maturity—and giving texture to the journey to the centerline in our model. The first window describes the *student,* young and excited about being on a journey to discover new things. In the second window, the *householder* marries, has children, develops an occupation, and makes money to support the family. The transition to the third window, the *forest-dweller,* initiates a further *inner* journey that is critical for moving close enough to the centerline to experience noticeable differences in our life with God. The forest-dweller leaves his or her self-defined security and occupation (not necessarily literally, but at least a delisting of career, titles, and achievements as the all-consuming focus of life) "to wander into bigger worlds" beyond existing paradigms—to be enlightened or discover what is real and what matters before it is too late. Finally, the fourth window depicts the *sage/holy person.* Being open to greater wisdom, the sage moves beyond a "me versus them" view of the world to a genuine love of others. The sage finds meaning and peace even in the midst of the trials of earthly life, and just by being the way they are brings light, hope, and strength to others. As these windows depict, *the journey to the centerline involves a reorientation of the human heart and life.* Which window best describes your life?

Importantly, the transforming journey to the centerline is fueled by the dynamic correspondence with God we have been discussing. This means making time to be still and training in basic skills for the spiritual life—such as discerning God's voice, prayer, bringing your heart into play, and engaging fruitfully in kingdom ministry—is fundamental to true discipleship. What training would help you move forward spiritually?

This pilgrimage to the centerline reflects the essence of a true biblical spiritual life and also the way of the Cross. Jesus taught, "Whoever wants to be my disciple must deny themselves and take up their cross daily and follow me" (Lk. 9:23). The disciple's pilgrimage to the centerline takes further shape if we can answer the question, "Why did Jesus take up his cross?" Jesus faced the suffering of Calvary to serve the purposes of God to save and restore the world. *So taking up our cross daily is to embrace whatever "sufferings" are required to participate with God in his restoration of our own lives and of all creation*—whatever it takes to transition us to a deeper acceptance and expression of God's will.

It is not suffering from our bad decisions; it is not suffering caused by unfulfilled self-centered demands; it is not suffering through religious hoop-jumping. Again, it is not suffering to be morally right—whipping ourselves to resist the world or praying because we feel obligated. No. *The sufferings Jesus talks about here are whatever it takes to make people glad in the goodness of God.* The sufferings required to move beyond just "licking the missions envelope" to living life-on-life with others in a way that befriends, heals, liberates, mercifully restores, saves and makes worshipers of them.

It may mean forfeiting the delights of sin or the self-gratifying pursuit of personal power. Giving up our right to vengeance and forgiving, or relinquishing self-condemnation to receive forgiveness, is "suffering" in this sense. Other examples include rejection when we witness, the price of offering friendship, making time when we are time-strapped, opening our homes to people on the periphery of our natural circle, and spending our energy on others beyond just ourselves and our own families. For my family, it meant having our car vandalized while participating in a kids' club in a rough neighborhood—part of the price of being in business with Jesus to bless our world. *Taking up our cross daily is the cost involved in hearing*

God speak and responding obediently to what we hear him saying to us. It is the cost of realizing the sacred life pressing against the seams of our souls for expression.

To grow spiritually or to move closer to God, by definition, means to love. And to love, by definition, means to give of the substance of our lives for others. What wonderful "suffering" if it saturates our lives in love, permits us a hands-on experience of God's in-breaking kingdom, and allows us the gift of some sort of union with God!

Someone might say, "Enough about cross-bearing! I'm struggling and need God." There are people who have been so smashed by life they need spiritual and emotional life-support. But Jesus consistently called people who were struggling and wanted a better life to follow him. *For Jesus, the journey to the centerline restores and releases the divinely inspired potential for a human life.* So why would we relegate struggling people to the "safe" margins, if not out of ignorance or some false sense of grace? Why would we ask for prayer repeatedly, but not also embrace a wider view of Christ's way to growth, wholeness, and healing—particularly if our current course is failing to deliver change or intimacy with God?

Inward Shifts

To make progress toward the centerline, some Christians simply need to embrace the biblical realities represented by our discipleship model, and genuinely try. But often trying harder is not enough. At some point, even exemplary followers require some "inward shifts" or changes in attitude to overcome internal obstacles to growth and pilgrimage.

A simple example of an "inward shift" would be to *let God love us.* To surrender the places hardened to God because of life's disappointments. Inwardly we shift from striving, covering up, resisting God, or attempting to earn his love, to admitting we are wrong, not the best, struggling, hurt, fearful, or jealous. The inward shift gives God entry to heal and love us. It gives him authority to speak into our lives, catalyzing the dynamic correspondence fueling the trek to the centerline. Do you need to make this inward shift?

Another example is to allow ourselves to *let it be personal with Jesus*. When Jesus called us to take up our cross "for his sake" (see Lk. 9:23), he was certainly making it personal. The inward shift is from making our faith about doctrine or right-doing, to making it about a relationship with Christ as a divine Person. Ignoring his words of love or being uninvolved in what he is doing is no longer inconsequential because it hurts *him*. Teresa of Avila taught that meditating upon the broken body of Christ, and letting his sacrifice get under our skin and into our hearts, is a significant step toward being drawn beyond ourselves.

As it is recorded in Luke 24, Jesus went to great lengths to dig the disciples out of the misconception he was a ghost—to shift their *attitude toward his resurrection*. But it still seemed too good to be true (they thought he was a ghost). We can change our attitude toward a person, and can also decide—by recalling our own experiences of God's grace and cranking open our minds using the inspired Scriptures—to shift our attitude toward Christ's Resurrection.[103]

Any move toward the centerline and union with God will require ongoing transformation because there is always some degree to which we are not like God. For this reason, *committing to being transformed* is an essential inward shift. We shift inwardly from pridefully thinking we are already spiritually mature to a humble commitment to lifelong learning, growing, and change. *We must commit to being transformed because we want more than a "nice friendship" with God.* Hannah Whitall Smith pointed out that in a "nice friendship," it is okay to spend a large part of our lives in separate interests and pursuits, but when friendship becomes love this changes. Separate interests and separate paths in life are no longer possible.

Things which were lawful before become unlawful now, because of the nearness of the tie that binds. The reserve and distance suitable to mere friendship becomes fatal in love. Love gives all and must have all in return. The wishes of one become binding obligations to the other, and the deepest desire of each heart is, that it may know every secret wish or longing of the other, in order that it may fly on the wings of the wind to gratify it.[104]

At the start Christ's disciples saw their need, believed and followed him, possessed great power to do his work, and saw amazing things, *but were unlike him*! They fought for top spot, misunderstood his mission, showed a lack of solidarity with others, and ran away from the Cross. But after Pentecost, there was no longer a war of wills and clashing interests; his will alone animated them. They had shifted inwardly and were more one with God. *To be one with God, it is not enough to say we love him; we must be transformed to share his priorities, interests, and vision.* How true is this of your own life?

It is natural to want a tidier program more under our control. But being spiritual midwives of the sacred life pressing to be birthed in us and others cannot be neatly captured in a four-week discipleship course. We must have robust faith and build a trellis to take us beyond adolescence and deeply into biblically defined spiritual reality—to find God, who is Spirit and Love.

For Discussion

1. Referencing the first five chapters, discuss the importance of spirituality for following Jesus. Do you think the spiritual aspects of your faith journey are strong enough?

2. Which of the five transitions explaining what discipleship must achieve impacted you the most, and why?

3. How do the distinctives of Christ's followers expressed in the Lord's Prayer challenge or inspire you?

4. Discuss how a synthesis of the two sides of the paradox we have been discussing is foundational for our model of discipleship.

5. Unpack the other elements and dynamics of the normal curve. (Include what the centerline represents, the journey to the centerline as the way of the Cross, and what it means to remain on the margins.) How does this help you to understand what it means to be Christ's disciple in the real world?

6. Why are inward shifts important for the journey of discipleship? Try to identify an inward shift from the examples given or elsewhere, that would assist your own pilgrimage to the centerline.

PART THREE

Strategies to Win the Will

CHAPTER 7

Spiritual Dullness
(The Devil's Strategy)

Satisfied with blindness,
but you pretend you want to see.

—TERRY TALBOT[105]

A little sleep, a little slumber, a little folding of the
hands to rest—and poverty will come on you like a
thief and scarcity like an armed man.

—PROVERBS 24:33–34

The Bible teaches that the devil has a strategy to sabotage all of our dynamic correspondence with God. He wants to deceive us into stopping responding to God until we become spiritually dull. Then, while God speaks words of love to us through the Bible and in our lives, we can't understand them in a way that frees us to respond. Our dynamic correspondence with God is hobbled at the knees, trapping us in a spiritual "holding pattern" marked by a wishy-washy expression of faith and a diminished experience of God.

In Andrew McDonough's children's book *Webster the Preacher Duck*, a flock of ducks waddle their way routinely every Sunday from the lake into church. Webster D. Duck, the world's greatest preacher, unpacks the truth God has given them wings so they can fly. "No more waddling; we'll fly to the moon and back!" his hearers enthusiastically reply. The church erupts in the "Hallelujah Chorus," thanking God they can fly in vee formation and participate in their migration. The ducks thank the preacher for a powerful message . . . and *waddle* their way routinely from the church back to the lake until next week.[106]

Fuzzy Faith

To attempt to fly and fall flat on your face is one thing, but to yearn to fly but be content with waddling—to have no inclination to try—is different. Many good Christians struggle to engage with God through the meat-and-potatoes expressions of their faith, such as prayer, reading the Bible, or witnessing. Time is an issue, but more, they just aren't meaningful or seen to be beneficial. Consequently, these Christians suffer a crisis of confidence about their ability to participate in the spiritual life. Their spiritual understanding is fuzzy, the pulse of true desire hard to find. Straightforward aspects of faith routinely become swamped amidst the busywork of life.

Fuzzy faith is behind our waddling ducks. God's revelation pours into their lives like water into a bucket with a hole in it. It elicits a momentary response, then drains away before it can transform them or satisfy their souls. They don't grow. Week after week, they waddle, remaining right where they are.

Can you identify with any of the following telltale signs?—reading the Bible and prayer are ho-hum; small talk is not about Jesus; church doesn't keep our attention; we are easily distracted; the Cross fails to move us; it feels as if God is in another cosmos; we champion issues that barely register (if at all) in the teaching of Jesus; despite right appearances, if we are honest, we just don't love what Jesus loves.

I hope not! But this is happening all around us.

Spiritual dullness doesn't make us wicked people or any less candidates for God's love, but it is spiritually debilitating. There will always be both passionate and indifferent followers of Christ in the church, but when fuzzy faith *defines* the church—when it characterizes a critical mass—we must take notice.

Being Un-born Again

Jesus told Nicodemus that to see and enter the kingdom of God we must be "born again" (see John 3:3). This involves a deep, inward change:

> The concept is of God renovating the heart, the core of a person's being, by implanting a new principle of desire, purpose, and action, a dispositional dynamic that finds expression in positive response to the gospel and its Christ. Jesus' phrase "born of water and the Spirit" (John 3:5) harks back to Ezekiel 36:25–27, where God is pictured as symbolically cleansing persons from sin's pollution (by water) and bestowing a "new heart" by putting his Spirit within them.[107]

It is not a religious ritual but an inward regeneration by the Holy Spirit by which a new, more vigorous and higher life is breathed into us (see Eph. 2:1–10). We are brought into a renewed existence in which we can discern the Christ, his love, power, and mission. We are liberated to hear and respond to God's words of love in Christ and to live in God's presence. It is a transition from spiritual death to spiritual life. Nicodemus was a good man and a religious ruler, but Jesus makes the point that the foundational essentials for life with God such as faith, repentance, and discipleship can't happen apart from this new birth. Spiritual dullness is spiritually devastating because it renders the believer effectively *un*-born again. In the same way any relationship suffers when neglected, when we neglect our involvement with God over time, love dies. We forget, and we no longer believe. I'm not talking about the status of salvation; I'm talking about the effect on our spiritual lives. *Spiritual dullness takes from us everything regeneration by the Holy Spirit gave to us.* This is the devil's strategy.

First, there can be no correspondence with God because we can't hear his voice, and so we forfeit the higher life in his presence. We may have the *forms* of correspondence—we understand that we should pray and we know God speaks—but these can simply deceive us into thinking we have the reality of the higher life when we don't. Despite the appearances, our existence is again governed by the voices of this fallen world and not by God's voice. It is Christianity putting on a brave face but without the assurance or motivation of true faith, without love, without authority and power, without grace, transformation, passion, or hope. We can't see the kingdom of God, and our engagement with him is so thin the Spirit could withdraw unnoticed.

Second, with regeneration comes a *call* to follow Jesus and find life, but spiritual dullness leaves us without the desire for it in any conscious, intentional, or active way. This is because the gospel no longer sets our hearts on fire; our hearts have lost the capacity to be illuminated about the personal importance of this message from God to us. Consequently, we don't serve the purposes of God much, or love Jesus much. After Jesus died Nicodemus and Joseph of Arimathea took risks to collect the body of Jesus from Pilate and lovingly wrap it, with spices, in strips of linen (see John 19:38–42). Nicodemus brought an extravagant amount of spices, as would be appropriate for a royal burial, but spiritual dullness takes away such love and service to King Jesus.

Being *un*-born again is the judgment of a lack of spiritual insight as the people in Isaiah's time experienced when they were consistently unresponsive to God's word. Isaiah describes their spiritual plight in terms of "ever hearing, but never understanding" (see Isaiah 6:9–10). Because of disuse their spiritual equipment for discerning God's voice became rusty and they heard the prophet's words but couldn't get the point; they looked to God but couldn't encounter him; and because they were spiritually deaf and blind they didn't turn to God so he could restore them.

A Devastating Blindness

Spiritual dullness builds up a buffer between us and the things we already know God wants us to do.

To be barefoot is to trust God's wisdom and the way of Jesus: the way to a wellspring in the dry field of a broken relationship is not revenge but forgiveness; the way past the emptiness of materialism is not to have more possessions but to not need them (Lk. 12:15); the way forward when success fails to make us happy is not to have more success but to learn how to love. To be barefoot is to obey Christ's call to love by laying down our lives and starting a dance party with the souls of others.

Whoever dodges following Jesus into a life of love *is already living out their judgment.* In time, they *cannot* hear or desire God enough to turn to him.

Discerning spiritual dullness can be tricky when we are spiritually dull. The symptoms mentioned in this chapter might help. An objective audit of our normal week to note consistent expressions of the sorts of things Jesus modeled— from receiving the Father's love on the mountainside to serving the poor—is a reasonable barometer. Do you suspect traces of spiritual dullness in your own life? Don't be shocked if you do because the sacred stream is evidently worth contesting in the spiritual realm. Take hope that, if even a flicker of desire remains, it is enough to be fanned through simple, consistent response to God's love and Word.

St. Francis of Assisi's Story

St. Francis, who founded the famous Franciscan missionary order, was an Italian traveling preacher who sought to imitate Jesus. He proclaimed the kingdom, called people to repentance and healed the sick. Francis subsisted on food handouts, and his kindness and love soon spread throughout Europe and the "little poor man" of Assisi became known as Saint Francis. [108]

As a young man, Francis worked for his father, a wealthy fabric merchant. His compassion was evident, but he mingled with nobles, and enjoyed boozy dances and partying. In 1202, he was taken prisoner while fighting bravely against Perugia in search of worldly glory and knighthood. After months of imprisonment he explained his cheerful attitude as resulting from his expectation that he would "one day be the idol of the whole world." On his release, Francis joined the struggles of the papal armies. He generously gave his extravagant garments to a knight with so little clothing he was almost naked. *The image of the God who is love presses through our dullness for expression; we all see its beauty and nobility, but dullness keeps us from understanding this as a way to live and be truly alive.*

One night while fighting for the papal armies a voice spoke to him in his sleep: ". . . why follow the servant, instead of the master on whom he depends?" He went home declaring he would still make it big but was a changed man. After a sumptuous banquet he was disgusted by his drunken friends and began to pray. Francis was so submerged in the sweetness of God's love that he appeared different to his friends:

> "What's wrong with you," they asked, "that you are not following us anymore? Are you planning to get married? And has your sweetheart turned your head?"

> "You are right!" replied Francis. "I *am* thinking of marrying! And the girl to whom I intend to plight my troth is so noble, so rich, and so good, that none of you ever saw her like!"[109]

His simple acts of involvement with God—such as returning home (he obviously thought God had spoken to him) and praying when revelry repulsed him—sharpened him spiritually; the muddle of his dullness crumbled, and he could discern the sweetness of God's love. Love radiated from him as a natural response. For example, he often spent time at a leper colony, distributing money to them, and "left only after kissing them all on the mouth."

We can't make Francis's exploits prescriptive, nor can we assume we will rendezvous with God in the same fashion. But like Francis, we can counter our own spiritual dullness with simple acts of involvement with God that position us for grace. Are you willing?

The Preacher's Dilemma

If we hear but disobey God's Word, listening to more preaching carries the risk of hardening our hearts more and more. This is a dilemma for discerning preachers. The prophet Isaiah's teaching, for example, was so simple and clear it was criticized as being fit for young children (see Isa. 28:9). The problem was not a lack of clarity, but too much light. When God's people in Isaiah's time persistently failed to *actually* do what God asked through the prophet, God's words became a curse. They brought the judgment expressed in Isaiah 6:9–10 that they would be "ever hearing, but never understanding." Because of disuse, their God-given heart equipment for hearing and responding to God became rusty and malfunctioned. Like our waddling ducks, we can (audibly) hear the best preaching in the world but not actually understand a fig of what God is saying to us!

We think we are hearing from God because we listen to a grade-A sermon or study the Bible, but we hear only information, not revelation, and we spiral spiritually downward and away from a dynamic correspondence with God.

Today there is a glut of God's Word through preaching, books, Bible studies, conferences, the Internet, and Christian radio and television. This torrent presents more opportunities to respond to God, but if we are not responsive—for whatever reasons—it can bring spiritual dullness.

Like the crowds milling around Jesus, we can observe miracles with our physical eyes but not perceive God. We can be stirred by truly excellent worship music but fail to "sing and make music in [our] heart to the Lord" (Eph. 5:19). We can wax lyrical about the preacher, the sermon, the miracle, the music, the worship leader, and perhaps even the experience, but with no stirring of allegiance for the Person to whom these things point. *Dull believers need "spiritual excellence" just to stay interested, but it doesn't do them any spiritual favors.*

We should encourage those who have divine grace to teach the Bible, lead worship in song, or do supernatural works, and thank God for them. But if (as I believe) a critical mass of Christians today is affected by spiritual dullness, we are facing the preacher's dilemma just as Isaiah did. "More and better" will bring judgment. *If we stack our conferences with A-list speakers without nurturing true work in the soil of the heart to enable response to God's Word we do believers a spiritual disservice.* The best seed in the world will struggle to take root or produce a crop, and soon we are spiritually dull. Our spiritual pulse might be lifted, but soon we are waddling again, having barely flapped our wings . . . until next time.

We must take responsibility for our own choices, but we can't discount the biblical truth that the devil is working to establish barriers in our minds against the knowledge of God (see 2 Cor. 10:4–5). If the devil blinds the minds of unbelievers so they cannot discern Christ (see 2 Cor. 4:4), it isn't a stretch to believe he will attack the minds of believers also. He will devour people by any means (see 1 Pet. 5:8). Christ was tempted by the devil to self-sufficiency, popularity, and power (see Matt. 4:1–11), and so are we today. In C. S. Lewis's allegorical tale *The Screwtape Letters*, the mercurial devil, Uncle Screwtape, instructs his nephew to *corrupt* his victim's spirituality if he can't remove it. Spiritual dullness invades our hearts by stealth to keep us from God's love and from God himself, and surely today the devil is subtly working every angle he can find.

Dullness in the New Testament

There are three direct references to Isaiah 6:9–10 in the Gospels that relate directly to critical aspects of discipleship, reinforcing how important it is that we understand and address the issue of dullness in the church.

MARK 4:11–12—DISCIPLES VS. CROWD

After teaching the parable of the sower to a large crowd by the lake, Jesus wrapped up the meeting and was alone with the Twelve *and the others*—those who wanted to stay involved with him and hung around. According to Jesus, they had been given the secret of the kingdom of God, but to the crowd (whose involvement with Jesus ended with the meeting), everything was said in parables so they might be "ever hearing but never understanding."

The "Principle of the Parable," he explained, is this: if for whatever reason you don't stick with God's Word—being continually open to it, working it out, allowing it to speak to you, and acting on it as the Spirit prompts—then Jesus, his mission, and the way of his kingdom will be like a parable or a confusing, perhaps boring, enigma.[110] Jesus is saying the seed (his Word) will die in the soil of our hearts and won't grow or bear fruit if we are hostile to, or not actively involved with, the Word and the Spirit. *Dullness is a natural consequence of the indifference that prevents us from hearing God's Word fully or in such a way that we are ready to obey.*

By accepting Christ, the seed of his life is planted in us (1 Pet. 1:23). The good soil nourishes the seed by *actively accepting* it; this distinguishes disciple from "crowd." Active acceptance means an attitude of belief and readiness to let it define us. It forms in us as we quiet ourselves and the Spirit waters the seed, connecting us with Christ's loving presence. Being barefoot in this way gives the seed a fighting chance to shoot its roots down into our souls, and to guide, heal, and grow us. *The more we are open to the kingdom life, the more we understand it and can enter it.* Otherwise, we are crowd. Our unwillingness makes for poor soil. The seed is prevented from putting down roots, or is choked by hardness or issues closing us to God's will and voice. Christ and his kingdom remain a distant puzzle. Mixing it with Jesus is not a real priority after the pizzazz of the weekly meeting is wrapped up because we are too dull to see the value of it, and we forfeit the opportunity of life with God beyond the flatland.

MARK 8:14–21—DULL DISCIPLES CAN'T FEED CROWDS

After Jesus miraculously fed two huge crowds of people with ridiculously small amounts of food, the Twelve quibbled about whether one loaf of bread would feed their entourage of thirteen. You do the math. Jesus warned them against the hypocrisy by which the Pharisees sought a sign but only as "spiritual sport," with no intention of believing in him. Similarly, the crowd lapped up the miracles and teaching of Jesus but without the reflection that would lead to faith. It was as if Jesus were saying to his disciples: "You had front row seats for two feeding miracles, but you seem dull like the Pharisees and crowd—as if you don't see me as the Messiah, or believe!"

He expected them to take some faith initiative and responsibility. At least they could have requested he pray over the loaf and do it again! He wasn't after heroics, but the spontaneous involvement in the kingdom that comes from true faith. Instead, like the crowd, their faith was *passive*. Earlier, Jesus had asked *them* to feed the crowd (see Mk. 6:37), but they complained about logistics rather than engaging in prayer. Jesus again quoted from Isaiah 6:9–10 to identify their failure to take faith initiative and responsibility as an issue of spiritual dullness.

You might make a list of examples from the last month when you have exercised faith initiative and responsibility.

The disciples participated with the Rabbi when he initiated kingdom activity, but otherwise they reverted to earthly things such as quibbling over a shortage of bread. This was important to Jesus because he was about to return to his Father, and if his disciples were too dull to take risks in faith to initiate kingdom activity, who would advance the kingdom after he was gone? If there is only crowd with no disciples, who can do anything more than "church jobs"? Who is going to do the work of Jesus? Who will feed the hungry people? As a Jesus-follower, will you?

JOHN 12:37–50—FASCINATION OR FAITH?

Jesus performed yet another miracle; the crowd was amazed—again—but they would not believe. John presents it as a case of spiritual dullness: Jesus demonstrated his divinity in front of their noses, but they couldn't see with their eyes or understand with their hearts. Their decision not to believe in the first place resulted in God's hardening their hearts, and for this reason they *could not* believe.

Fascination is not the same as faith (or following). Both are a type of commitment, but the goal of the first is only to gawk at or receive something, while the second is the abandonment of confidence in ourselves. It is to respond by seeking *him*, yielding control, following, and serving. Jesus pointed out to the fascinated crowd that his words come from the Father and lead to eternal life; for that reason, those who hear him and don't obey choose judgment for themselves (see John 12:44–50).

Fascination is fatal because we think we are committed (when we are not) in such a way that Jesus will entrust himself to us in a real relationship. This was the type of commitment that followed a highly successful time of ministry for Jesus while he was in Jerusalem for Passover (see John 2:23–25). John writes, "[M]any people saw the signs he was doing and believed in his name." They made a decision of faith *because* they saw the miraculous signs Jesus was doing, or *so long as* they were seeing them.[111] We might be tempted to be happy with this result, but Jesus wasn't. He doesn't treat this as real faith, and certainly not as deep faith. He sees it as fickle puppy love, the stuff of first attraction that knows what Jesus does but doesn't really know *him* yet. Because of this, it is a wobbly faith still at risk of being overthrown by the next attraction. Luther called it "milk faith," held by those who quickly and enthusiastically give in and believe, but just as quickly withdraw when they hear something that doesn't tickle their fancy. Jesus saw right through this sort of "young" faith.

The kingmakers who tried to coronate Jesus by force (see John 6:14–15) did so because his miraculous feeding of the five thousand had their minds whirling with the idea he was a messiah like a super-Spartacus,[112] who would oust the Romans and serve their earthly interests. Following his life of sacrifice and love as the way to God and spiritual renewal just wasn't on their radar. They completely missed what Jesus was about, and he had to get away from them. Is *our* commitment the sort that invites Jesus to come to us—or the sort that turns him away? The more our commitment serves earthly interests, the less he can trust us in a relationship—not because he loves us any less for it, but because we won't build a life around the trek with him toward love and God.

The fascination that characterizes spiritual dullness won't lead to discipleship or a naturally supernatural life, but only to more spectators.[113] This is because real spiritual authority comes from intimacy with Christ (see Matt. 28:18). It works through the genuine love formed as we authentically relate to him, not just by experiencing the supernatural. Fascination poses the danger of pursuing sanctification by supernatural experience in place of a dynamic correspondence with God.[114] Fascinated believers don't really respond to *Jesus*; they simply come back for more signs.

While spiritually mature followers obviously experience and are conduits of God's supernatural grace in wonderful ways, the Bible teaches true spiritual maturity is evidenced by love (and the other fruits of the Spirit), obedience, and witness. *Spiritual gifts are invaluable tools servicing these markers.*

Believers fascinated with Anthony of the Desert's teaching came to him and said:

> "Speak a word; how are we to be saved?" The old man said to them, "You have heard the Scriptures. That should teach you how." But they said, "We want to hear from you too, Father." Then the old man said to them, "The Gospel says, 'if anyone strikes you on one cheek, turn to him the other also'" (Matt. 5:39). They said, "We cannot do that." The old man said, "If you cannot offer the other cheek, at least allow one cheek to be struck." "We cannot do that either," they said. So he said, "If you are not able to do that, do not return evil for evil," and they said, "We cannot do that either." Then the old man said to his disciples, "Prepare a little brew of corn for these invalids. If you cannot do this, or that, what can I do for you? What you need is prayers."[115]

The sick rightly hunt for God's healing power with every breath (and we should do it with them), but the antidote for fascination is not more signs. It is prayer, rethinking the real nature of our commitment and being honest about the kind of power we are seeking—whether we seek God's pleasure and glory or our own.

Climbing Out of the Dullness Ditch

If you can identify with some of the symptoms of being stuck in the dullness ditch this is a great start to climbing out. Now, size up what we have discussed in this chapter about the biblical reality of spiritual dullness, and make a clear-cut, nitty-gritty decision to find ways to start corresponding with God. *If spiritual dullness pounces when our correspondence with God is compromised, it makes sense that reinstating basic involvement with God provides footholds out of the ditch.*

Your efforts may be uninspired at first, but persevere with the reassurance that the glowing embers of your desire to climb out of the ditch can be fanned into flame even if the wood is fairly damp. God and grace are everywhere, and it's not that hard to get wet in the ocean if you try! God doesn't need his arm twisted to reveal his love; all he is waiting for is some sort of authentic movement toward him. In this way, hunger (even a "grit your teeth because there isn't much hunger" decision) begets more hunger.

We should find further encouragement in the fact that God too has a strategy in place to contend for our wills—the instruction of our hearts by the Holy Spirit. But before we discuss God's strategy, we are going to look at the human strategy to win us over by artificially impassioning our hearts. As Webster D. Duck discovered, this is no true remedy at all against unwillingness for the life of love.

For Discussion

1. Do you struggle to engage with God through the basic expressions of faith, such as prayer, reading the Bible, or witnessing? Why do you think this is the case?
2. What is spiritual dullness? How do you think this applies to your spiritual life today?
3. What could you identify with in the story of Francis of Assisi?
4. If it is true that God's Word becomes a curse when we are persistently unresponsive to it, explain how you think this might change the way you think about listening to sermons or utilizing other Christian resources.

5. To what extent do you believe the devil is deceitfully weaning believers away from God's way? Discuss how you think this is happening today and the consequences for your own life.

6. Explain the "Principle of the Parable" from Mark 4:11–12. Do you think you are a disciple or one of the crowd? Why?

7. Why is faith initiative and responsibility important in the kingdom life? Does this come naturally for you or is it difficult? Explain.

8. In what ways is fascination not the same as faith, and how does this distinction challenge you? (Note how Jesus responded to the fascinated crowd in John 12:44–50.)

CHAPTER 8

Artificial Impassioning
(Human Strategy)

A man convinced against his will is
of the same opinion still.

—ANONYMOUS[116]

The devil's strategy derails our responsiveness to God's Word and renders us spiritually dull. Human strategy is to provide external motivations for us to do things. This can produce fast results, but not the depth God imagines for us.

Not All Passion Works the Same Way

To be impassioned is good, but not all passion works the same way. The birthplace of our desire is important for an authentic, spontaneous response to God. When believers are unresponsive, there are two options open to them and their leaders. The first is to wind *down* to the still, quiet place of the heart and to enable the Holy Spirit to reveal God's love there. This mirrors the teaching of Jesus that kingdom living flows from the heart, or from the inside out. If you like, this is to be properly impassioned or impassioned in an enduring way. The second option, a much more natural tendency, is to wind *up,* stirring passions and exciting from the outside in. This artificial attempt to sway the will can only result in artificial desire because our will is not altered; human beings do not have the power to renovate the human heart. We are simply enticed—*against* our will by external "bait." How dependent is your Christian involvement on external activity?

At bedrock, God isn't after our responses per se, as if he needs our help or flattery. He is, however, seeking our involvement with him as an expression of genuine desire and, therefore, worship. For this reason, it is absurd to entertain the idea God would be satisfied with our responses—even responses that serve his purposes—if they were propped up by some other external motivation. He can certainly *use* such responses, but how he interprets them relationally is another issue (see Matt. 7:21–23).

Jesus Pushed for a Proper Exercise of the Will

Jesus left little doubt about the significance he placed on choosing *inwardly* for God instead of pretending with external pious appearances when our heart is against God. His stand on this issue attracted more hostile response than any other, and it is why in John 7 we learn that Jesus went up to Jerusalem secretly for the Feast of Tabernacles.

With the Feast in full swing, Jesus surfaced to teach in the temple courts, and his hearers questioned his teaching credentials. He retorted,

> My teaching is not Mine, but His who sent Me. If anyone is willing to do His will, he will know of the teaching, whether it is of God or whether I speak from Myself (John 7:16–17 NASB).

His point: if we are "willing" to obey God, we will have the capacity to discern whether the words of Jesus come from God or from man. *By actively accepting or being sincerely open to his teaching and turning inwardly toward Jesus (unlike his hearers), we can hear his teaching in the sense that it is meaningful, and respond to it.* But artificial or external impassioning doesn't make us any more sincere toward God; it might stir our emotions, but it can't transform our heart.

The Greek verb used in John 7:17 for "willing" in this context (root word *thelo*) means to exercise the will properly by an operation, *not to be artificially impassioned by external means.* It is to want, and actually intend, to do the will of God. We might even be awful in the doing, but we are inclined toward it like a sprinter set toward the finish line by our inner choice. "Willing" here is not just ethical determination but involves faith[117]—to believe in the one God has sent; to choose inwardly those things he teaches and loves.

The point Jesus makes can be illustrated by thinking about receiving divine revelation from reading a book. If we are hungry for God to speak and believe he will, even bad books or secular books can enlighten us. If not, a profoundly spiritual book might not take us any further, because we will hear only what we want to hear.

The crowd in the frame of John 7 tests the competence of Jesus as a teacher, and he then questions *their* competence as hearers. We often think receiving communication is passive. As two great experts on reading and comprehending what we read explain it, "The mistake here is to suppose that receiving communication is like receiving a blow or a legacy or a judgment from court. On the contrary, the reader or listener is much more like the catcher in a game of baseball. Catching the ball is just as much an activity as pitching or hitting it."[118]

Jesus only considers his hearers to be competent if they hear with an attitude of openness to receive and a readiness to act. *He teaches here that wanting to do God's will leads to spiritual enlightenment, but artificially impassioned willingness does not.* Authentic desire energizes us to involve with God and to seek him—the key to finding. But artificial impassioning distracts us from God by appealing to our ego or just fails to energize us toward God's love or presence because it is powerless to renovate the heart.

Nonetheless, our churches too often persist in motivating believers *externally.* With this in mind, think about the way your own faith community operates.

Trading Biblical Goals for Something Else

"Great holes!" my neighbor exclaimed, peering into the neat row of meter-deep holes along the perimeter of my backyard. The holes were bored into the almost impregnable clay by an auger attached to a tractor, and had an impressive semblance of art about them. I explained my vision of build a retaining wall, but my neighbor seemed more preoccupied with the holes.

White-hot biblical priorities requiring work in the heart can be subtly drowned out by good (but not central) things achievable through human effort. Musical excellence drowns out spiritual worship. Inviting people to church replaces Spirit-empowered witness. Getting people *in* substitutes for taking people *on.* Can you see how the "good thing" nudges the focus toward the church operation, while the white-hot priority serves the kingdom?

When we trade core biblical priorities for something less, we will tend toward artificial impassioning with immediate results. Discerning Christians, however, will be aware of the impact of this dynamic on their spiritual journey. When our behavior is motivated by external influences our primary response is not to Christ at all. We give our lives to Jesus *on our terms,* but this is spiritually devastating, because Jesus said that accepting *his* terms is the highway to God.[119]

One attempt at shifting the terms of the deal is the offer of rewards: roles making us feel significant, adulation before the crowd, the kudos of being part of an elite in-group. Promises of material blessing fit this bill too, as do guarantees of a trouble-free life. Also, the assurance we can be gods of our own private lives—in other words, we can do what we like with our own time, energy, and money. On top of this, entertainment is assured (including a dose of humor in the message), as is attachment to an exciting enterprise—a dose of the supernatural or a burgeoning missions program. Services are provided to help us parent and budget. We are thanked for attending church, like valued customers at McDonald's.

The terms of the contract subtly shift our way, impoverishing the soil of our hearts so that God's Word struggles to take root and our responsiveness is feeble. This is spiritual suicide!

In contrast, Jesus didn't balk at making his terms crystal clear, knowing many would reject him. In fact, he saw himself as an obstacle, a rock of offense, that stood in the way of blessing (see Matt. 11:6). He allowed people to stumble at his terms and fall away rather than compromise (see John 6:53–69). Jesus took the standpoint that nobody *must* follow him, but anybody *can* as a gift of grace. It wasn't that his terms kept people from the reality of his kingdom, but that they couldn't "see" him. *Having the discernment to delight in Christ's tough terms is pure mercy.*

The "Weakness" of God

God has chosen to vest great power in what seems to be weak. For example, he used a youngster hurling a stone to defeat a giant, and a march around Jericho to topple its walls. Jesus gave up his glory to come to earth, modeled meekness and love as the key to revolution, hung around with outcasts, shunned worldly power and earthly possessions, made time to linger in solitude on a mountainside, and sacrificed his life to save people who didn't even like him.

How have you embraced what seems "weak" in the Jesus-life?

Artificial impassioning exposes the temptation of the church to, like the Corinthian believers, try to curry favor with God by our brilliance, earnings, anointing, achievements (even in ministry), possessions, physical beauty, or influence. But God chooses "nobodies" and makes use of ways considered weak in worldly circles, so there is absolutely no confusion about who should be worshiped (1 Cor. 1:27–29).

The Holy Spirit must enlighten us to see the power God has vested in what seems weak and foolish (see 1 Cor. 2:14). Sure-fire formulas for outward success must give way to the vigor of the battle for the heart.

The way of Jesus is scandalous to many Western believers because a devotion to human interests has a white-knuckle hold on our prevailing worldview. Self-gratification and entertainment are central, and the individual is treated as god. It's possible to believe in the God of the Bible but still be enslaved by this worldview. *Acting for our own gratification is our natural default unless we intentionally pursue a redefining of our worldview toward biblical and kingdom values.*

This explains why many Western Christians live for self-satisfaction through the accumulation of material things, or commit to something or someone (including marriage partners and churches) only as long as they entertain or make them happy. It also explains why appealing to such human interests makes churches numerically successful.

Teresa of Avila describes the blessing of the call to die to self in terms of the transformation of a silkworm into a beautiful butterfly.[120] Like the silkworm, when the season is right, mature believers choose to spin Christ's life around themselves, building a cocoon in which they will die to self-love, self-will, and the attachment to earthly things. A new, larger-than-life existence with Christ in God now emerges (see Col. 3:3). It is *her* life, symbolized by the flight, color, and beauty of the emerging butterfly. Death is the prerequisite for new and sacred life, but this is foolishness to those devoted to human interests.

The Way In Is the Way On

Unless Jesus (on his terms) is the entry point in the sense of the narrow gate (see Matt. 7:13–14), our churches will spend the bulk of their budgets on artificially impassioning us just to keep us. If the music initially attracted us, or the scope of the operation— friendships, entertaining sermons, promises of significance, or the supernatural—then these things must be dished up consistently to hold our interest and keep us coming. A flurry of church activity simply maintains us in some sort of pre-commitment stage.

External impassioning will always debilitate the spiritual life by supplying a surrogate for the pursuit of inward desire, the spiritual X factor for corresponding dynamically with God. Shifting terms is just one of the dynamics at work to impassion the will externally. The following are some others.

Idealism

In *Renegotiating the Church Contract,* James Thwaites identifies an idea of Plato's that affects the thinking of the church today: that a perfect or ideal spiritual realm (heaven) exists, and is separate and distinct from the natural, created realm of everyday life.[121] The corollary is we save people *out* of the world so they can enter heaven in the *next* life. Importantly, access to sacred life centers heavily around participation in the formal or organized activities of the church.

The Bible offers a different view: we can know God in *this* life through obedience in our everyday relationships and work (see Col. 1:9–10); this is where a dynamic correspondence with God finds its fulfillment. But church culture squeezes our effective God-involvement down to fit its own activities and then dangles the ideal of the perfect spiritual state before us, so like a mouse on a treadmill we keep running, or engaging in the formal activities of the church, for fear that we will miss out on the prize. But it always remains beyond us. Does this resonate with your experience?

> [Idealism] declares that reality is not you, it's not the place you occupy, it's not at this time, it's not the spotted desires of your fragile and fallen heart—it's somewhere, someone, something, sometime other. It's when you are strong enough, when you are pure enough, when you have enough, when you die and go to heaven. It's when you rise to fame, when you own this, when you can do that, when you are like this—whatever, it's just not you, it's just not here and it's just not now. And because it's not you it must come from elsewhere. . . . It might be the church you attend where you can identify with the dynamic leader who has special access to the realm ever beyond you. It might be the body of knowledge you must have to give your life the (ideal) definition you need to break through or at least feel secure. It might be the anointing that will one day come if you have enough faith to deserve it. It might be a perfect moral state that you will one day attain to if you keep thinking, adjusting and performing the right way. Until the time that the ideal arises to conquer your present half-life, you need to keep taking the cure, keep performing, keep trying, keep giving, keep attending, keep obeying. Don't ever give up, because one day you will be "there." [122]

Believing in and serving the institution and its ideals is confused with believing in and serving Christ. Faith is not in Christ at all, but in faith itself—reconfigured into X number of steps toward an aspect of the ideal. Believers are being impassioned by idealism.

Corporate Identity

For a corporate identity to motivate, it must attach people to a "happening thing"—visible results or something big, powerful, and energizing.[123] This is why the church, when influenced by construct dynamics tends toward extending *itself*. Even missions, evangelism, worship music, education, and childcare can serve this end.

Attaching ourselves to something successful is one way of satisfying the ache in our souls for significance. We are the parent of the kid who won the race, or we attend the church that hosted the well-known speaker or does groundbreaking missions work (though we wouldn't go ourselves). *The things to which we attach ourselves become part of our own identity.* If the church succeeds, we do also. This motivates us to attend and to serve the rise of this big, successful thing, that becomes our spiritual universe doling out opportunity and significance. Can you see this happening to you?

The Hebrew approach to the individual is reflected in the New Testament idea that every believer has a unique design and purpose (see Eph. 2:10). The parts are not swallowed up by the body—together they form it. *Christ is our corporate identity, and the church is a corporate entity only because individual believers are united with one heart by their love for him* (see Eph. 4:11–16). This corporate dynamic *empowers* the pilgrimage of individuals rather than swallows it.

Are you able to identify your unique design and purpose as an individual apart from the church organization?

Sociological Techniques

American journalist and Pulitzer Prize-winning author Thomas Friedman said, "Tap into people's dignity, and they'll do anything for you. Ignore it, and they won't lift a finger."[124] One example is the use of flattery to gratify people's vanity. My wife received a printed birthday card from a church where she attended a conference, saying she was an "amazing, godly, and beautiful woman." All those things are true, but the card was sent by people who don't know her from a bar of soap! Again, it taps into a biblical truth, but it honors people in a false way. Flattery *takes*—it wants something in return (in this case, attendance at the next conference). It is like carnal love that loves to be loved.

Another sociological technique used to impassion people externally is responding to trends in society. For example, age-old wisdom from Jesus rallying us to be generous to the poor and fight for justice has recently moved into vogue in parts of the church. Why now? I believe it is because it is now a trend in society. A well-known psychologist in Melbourne, Australia, prescribed a weekly program of charitable activities to revitalize the souls of highly successful clients coming to him in midlife, feeling empty. A reality TV offering in Australia was *Random Acts of Kindness*, and the Australian *Reader's Digest* cited research showing altruism is a powerful catalyst for happiness. Something that has always been crystal clear in Christ's teaching is now an effective external motivation for church involvement. This looks like discipleship but it is sociology.

Out of Nothing

Ex nihilo is a Latin term meaning "out of nothing." God created ex nihilo, reminding us he is sovereign and worthy of worship. Jesus held off until no doubt remained that Lazarus was dead before resurrecting him *out of nothing* to emphasize God's glory (see John 11:4, 14–15). It is from *nothing*—rather than the *something* created by external impassioning—that God will show his glory.

Biblically and throughout history God has spoken and acted powerfully at times, and been quiet at others. I was present in the early 1970s in parts of Papua New Guinea as God wonderfully manifested his presence. Where my father was ministering, incredible numbers of people were baptized. However, Miss Hackett, an elderly spinster who was a missionary there, had prayed for decades for that revival because the village was in a spiritual drought. She knew what to do in a lull, and it wasn't to play God.

The temptation in a lull is to orchestrate a result by our own strength. The first spiritual minefield involves muscling in on God's glory. Second, artificial impassioning fills the *nothing* out of which God creates. It is a critical *nothing* in which God tests our integrity and prepares our hearts in the valley of humility for the better blessings of his *something*.[125] Ebb and flow provides the texture and meaning to any real relationship. However, the *nothing* becomes so unbearably painful or costly to our reputation, that we hack the ball off the tee before God can have his shot. How have you been tempted to do this?

Firsthand Involvement

Dull believers too often subsist vicariously through exciting pastoral leaders and special services, but *escaping dullness demands we find ways to deepen our own involvement with God.* Christians are no more likely to get spiritually fit by participating vicariously from the stands than Olympic spectators are likely to get physically fit by watching Ian Thorpe swim.

We won't catapult ourselves into sacred space overnight. Initially, we might simply open our hearts to what the Bible says about God's love for us and allow ourselves to be truly thankful in response. Over time we gradually build the depth and breadth of our firsthand involvement with God.

For example, we register someone else's discoveries preached in a sermon at one level, but self-discovered truth explodes in the bunkers of our soul, mobilizing us inwardly to respond to God and join him in his kingdom work (see John 5:19). Again, when we share the gospel *ourselves* we dip our hearts in the sweetness of God's transforming love in Christ.

Nobody can find God, experience his love, worship him, or respond to him for us. *The journey to God is wonderfully and lovingly personal, and firsthand involvement with his Word and Spirit is basic to it.*

What steps are you willing to take toward a deeper, firsthand involvement with God?

Many believers in the church remain spiritually poor because they are not empowered to become involved in a firsthand way with God.

[I]t is no wonder that people grow passive, lethargic, and irresponsible. Why should the laity put forth any effort when their leaders will do it for them? Why should they develop skills of critical thinking and spiritual discernment when they can hire professionals instead? [Treating believers like children] perpetuates immaturity and thus dependency in followers.[126]

In what ways do you embrace the responsibilities of a spiritual adult, and where is growth needed?

Ancient Israel's Year of Jubilee outrageously expressed God's grace by recalibrating life back to a level playing field to allow everyone a fresh start under the rhythms of God's heart. Church leaders must dare to do likewise by relinquishing their power to artificially impassion people. In the pews, we must assume responsibility for casting off the spiritually false system of living out our faith vicariously—along with our expectations of being entertained and spiritually propped up—and resolve to invest in a firsthand correspondence with God. This way God can instruct our hearts by the Holy Spirit, win over our wills to make us "barefoot," and liberate us (individually and corporately as churches) toward love and himself—which, of course, is the point.

For Discussion

1. Do you think your church is focused more on winding *down* to the heart to enable the Holy Spirit's work there, or winding *up* by trying to motivate believers externally? Why do you think it matters?

2. Discuss the teaching of Jesus recorded in John 7:16–17. Why did Jesus push for an inward choice to do God's will, and how is our competence as hearers important?

3. Describe a way in which you think you try to shift Christ's terms. Why do you think we do this when blessing is found in the grace to accept his terms?

4. How does the "weakness" of God impact our involvement with him? Discuss the following statement: "We can believe in the God of the Bible but be devoted to human interests in our worldview."

5. Discuss how *idealism, corporate identity,* and *sociological techniques* are distorting your spirituality.

6. Why does living out our faith vicariously keep us spiritually dull? Using practical examples, ask yourself how vicarious is your own life of faith. Why is *firsthand* involvement with God important?

CHAPTER 9

Heart Instruction by the Holy Spirit (God's Strategy)

I keep asking that the God of our Lord Jesus Christ, the glorious Father, may give you the Spirit of wisdom and revelation, so that you may know him better. I pray that the eyes of your heart may be enlightened in order that you may know the hope to which he has called you, the riches of his glorious inheritance in his holy people.

—EPHESIANS 1:17–18

Human strategy leaves us still asking, "But how does God's love become real? How can we move beyond blind belief and doggedly doing Christian things, to passionate hunger for God and the way of Jesus? Where is the spiritual spark?" God's answer, his strategy to win over our will, is to light up our heart with knowledge of his love by the Holy Spirit.

Our Heroes Had Help

In the third century, Cyprian, the Bishop of Carthage, wrote about an uncommon quality of life:

> I have discovered . . . a quiet and holy people, who have learned a great secret. They have found a joy which is a thousand times better than any of the pleasures of our sinful life. They are despised and persecuted, but they care not. They are masters of their souls. They have overcome the world. These people, Donatus, are Christians . . . and I am one of them.

Unlike Cyprian's Christians, our souls are restless, and the challenges of the world seem to have our measure and distract us from God. But before we abandon the hope of emulating our heroes of faith, the Bible tells us these were not "better believers"—God supernaturally instructed their hearts. Precisely for this reason, they did the things to which we aspire.

For example, Moses took flight from Egypt, then returned to set the Israelites free because "he saw him who is invisible" (Heb. 11:27b). The disciples who bumped into Jesus on the road to Emmaus returned to Jerusalem with rekindled faith because "their eyes were opened and they recognized him" (Lk. 24:31). The first disciples of Jesus abandoned everything to join his circle because they discerned something of his divine identity (see Lk. 5:4–11). Jesus described the kingdom in terms of a merchant who found a pearl and sold everything to buy it because he "saw" its immense value (see Matt. 13:45–46).

God graciously "works in [us] to will and to act in order to fulfill his good purpose" (Phil. 2:13). Thankfully he doesn't intend us to do this without spiritual wisdom and understanding or the revelation of his love. Searching for it like a treasure-hunter is a normal part of biblical spirituality[127] because we cannot expect a fruitful pilgrimage or a kingdom life without spiritual intelligence.

In what ways are you intentional about seeking enlightenment from God?

Instruction of the Heart

For the apostle Paul, the secret to being a genuine Jew (or we could say, Christian) is to "know his will and approve of what is superior because you are instructed by the law" (Rom. 2:18). In other words, the law was to impart spiritual "smarts" to the heart about God and his superior way of love, energizing God's people to desire it and live it. The Jews clutched the law in their hands, but would not be instructed by the spiritual knowledge and truth it embodied.

In this sense, the law is not just a list of rules but an accomplice of grace. Against its Old Testament background, *law* means "teaching." It is what caring parents impart to their beloved children (e.g., Prov. 4:1–4; 7:1–3).[128] The Ten Commandments resonate with the rhythm of God's love, and the law was to impart that rhythm to the human heart to liberate it toward God and his life of love (see Rom. 13:8–10).

When we allow the pulsating rhythm of God's law to permeate the core of our being we are transformed in the same way as people who start tapping their feet and moving to the beat of music. We are moved by the sacred beat of his merciful love: to acceptance, forgiveness, hope, justice, peace, generosity, worship, holiness, providing for the poor, joy, salvation and restoration. Stepping to this rhythm of love *is* salvation and the kingdom. It is our God-imagined life.

So Paul can say . . . "clothe yourselves with the Lord Jesus Christ" (Rom. 13:14), meaning to wear his truth or vibe on the inside, in our spirits. Can you identify one way Christ's truth or vibe has come alive in you recently?

Rhythm or Rules?

No one is twisting our arm to cling to the Bible and the teachings of Jesus, but if we do, we have two options. The first is to whole-heartedly welcome its rhythm and beat as a foundation for our earthly existence—a no-compromise, all-of-life invasion of God's love, ways, thinking, priorities, and purpose even if our execution is deplorable. The second option is to humor it, embracing just enough to stay religiously viable.

When Paul says, "If you are led by the Spirit, you are not under law" (Gal. 5:18), he is not saying we escape the law. Rather, if our hearts are instructed by the Spirit and we resonate with the rhythm of the law, we won't be under the hammer of its rules. The law will be our delight (see Ps. 1:2) and the theme of our song (see Ps. 119:54). We will run in the path of God's commands because he has liberated our heart to its rhythm (see Ps. 119:32).[129] This is God's strategy.

After hearing the story of a Christian couple who found joy in adopting nine unwanted children with complicated medical problems, an unsaved man, fighting off tears, said, "It's beautiful." True freedom is not being freed *from* the law but being freed *into* its beautiful rhythm with bells on! Christ's life is a *Beautiful Life*.

Do you feel that you are under God's law as if it is a heavy burden? Could this be because you resist its rhythm?

New Understanding to Live in

Jesus offers a bit of mysticism when he says, "No one knows the Son except the Father, and no one knows the Father except the Son and those to whom the Son chooses to reveal him" (Matt. 11:27b). As we "come" to Christ, the Holy Spirit guides us into the inner circle of understanding with the Father and Jesus—an understanding of the Beautiful Life. By grace, we enter God's world, or the way he sees things, prioritizes things, and does things. *We acquire not just knowledge about God, but new understanding to live in.* This explains the vigorous faith and enduring peace and joy of our biblical heroes even in impossible difficulty. And for this reason Horatio Spafford could pen the hymn "It Is Well With My Soul" after his four beloved daughters drowned crossing the Atlantic Ocean by ship in 1873.

One day fishing for a much-prized red emperor on a reef in Papua New Guinea, my hook kept getting snagged in coral. A local friend started beating the top of the water with roots gathered from a nearby tree. A milky substance (a mild anesthetic) colored the water, and soon we could grab the fish with our hands. This was the power of the deeper understanding and practices of my friend's culture. In the same way, living in God's understanding of things is fundamental to the deeper life in God. *Discipleship is the process by which we can live well because the understanding underpinning Christ's life becomes more natural and beautiful to us* (see Matt. 11:29).

A Fresh Angle on Eternal Life

Just before his arrest Jesus prayed, "Now this is eternal life: that they may know you, the only true God, and Jesus Christ, whom you have sent" (John 17:3). It is striking that eternal life is not framed in terms of a legal transaction (e.g., the blood of Jesus paid off the debt for our sin and so we will have eternal life, as true as this is), but in terms of a relationship with God based on spiritual knowing. Think for a minute about this shift in perspective.

The Greek verb for "know" here is *ginosko,* meaning much more than knowing intellectually. It's the sort of knowing found in an intimate relationship—the ongoing, increasing knowing of a person in the heart. Let's try to apply this to knowing God. Using the same word, *ginosko,* Jesus says, "You will know the truth, and the truth will set you free" (John 8:32). It is not just truth, but *knowing* truth in a specific way that sets us free. It means to learn, understand, or to "put on" truth and the knowledge of God by the Holy Spirit—to be inwardly instructed by the truth. The Bible teaches our hearts can know things our minds can miss, and some amount of spirituality is required to guide us beyond our limited intellect. To know God in this deeper, spiritual way is transforming and swings open the door to a different quality of life.[130] This is possible because, after accepting Christ, we can continue to grow in spiritual understanding of him in a way that heals, liberates, and empowers us.

For most people true conversion takes place over time as we come to know (*ginosko*) God's love in Christ, and as we respond his tastes, priorities, worldview, authority, and love are woven into the fabric of our heart DNA by the Spirit. The by-product is an uncommon quality of living or blessedness called "eternal life."

While in a personal valley myself, I once "stumbled" upon Psalm 142:3: "When my spirit grows faint within me, it is you who watch over my way." I wrote in my journal: "Between the lines of this verse, I hear a whisper that words cannot express—a whisper of love and security. A whisper from the depths of what God knows to the depths of my soul, restoring rest." By reading between the lines and listening with our heart, we experience little (and sometimes big) *knowings*—we hear God. We connect with his presence in the world, dipping into the sweetness of his greater life. Can you recall a personal experience of this sort of spiritual knowing?

This is mainstream biblical practice, not some mystical sideshow. Heart instruction by the Holy Spirit enables the Christian to enter Christ's peace, to practice his virtues, and to do his works—both practical and supernatural. We don't just possess revelation, but it blesses us with rightly ordered desires that liberate us to authentically echo the revolutionary Jesus-life in the practical aspects of everyday life.

The Divine Instructor

God is spirit, and there is no escaping this "knowing" happens as we relate to him *in spirit*. People can instruct our minds (our intellect), but only the Holy Spirit can instruct our hearts (or spiritual mind) concerning the deepest things about God and ourselves (1 Cor. 2:14). The Holy Spirit's testimony about Jesus sparked an inward fire in the believers who revolutionized their world post-Pentecost. Their lives fulfilled Old Testament prophecies about the new covenant in Christ:

> I will put my law in their minds and write it on their hearts. I will be their God, and they will be my people . . . they will all know me. . . (Jer. 31:33b, 34b).

> I will give them an undivided heart and put a new spirit in them; I will remove from them their heart of stone and give them a heart of flesh. Then they will follow my decrees and be careful to keep my laws. They will be my people, and I will be their God (Ezek. 11:19–20).

God's heart still beats strongly for a "barefoot" people willing to obey him because his law is inscribed on their hearts by the Holy Spirit.

Paul prayed for the "Spirit of wisdom and revelation" to enable the Ephesians to know (*ginosko*) God better and to enlighten the eyes of their heart to know (*oida*, meaning to see in the sense of perceiving) the blessedness of life with God (see Eph. 1:17–19). *Because the Holy Spirit floods our heart with light, our life with God takes on meaning, hope, and power.* God enlightens. Our part is to orient our lives toward God as a faith-filled response. For Richard Foster, our part involves spiritual disciplines: "We are simply finding ways to place who we are—body, mind, and spirit—before God. All of this, I must add, flows out of the proper disposition of heart: seeking first the kingdom of God, hungering and thirsting for righteousness, longing to be like Christ."[131] What is the disposition of your heart?

Nobody else can place our true selves before God through first-hand involvement with his Word and Spirit because they are not us—our heart resides in *us*. If we are slack with this because time is short, or we don't have a handle on the "how," the revelation of preachers, writers, and those graced to prophesy will not instruct our hearts, or even our intellect, in any way that matters.

A Practical Primer

Someone once said to me, "I want a deeper spiritual life, but whatever I do just doesn't feel very deep." Sadly, this is a common feeling, and while a spiritual life is fundamental to life with God, it doesn't happen automatically when we are saved. *Our challenge is to identify ways to position ourselves so God can instruct our heart.* I would now like to get us thinking about the more practical aspects of this challenge.

James, the brother of Jesus, wrote: "Come near to God and he will come near to you" (James 4:8). The coming near to God part is our responsibility, but we cannot determine when, or how, or how much we will encounter God. We must simply persevere doing our part, full of faith that, if we seek, we will find (see Matt. 7:7). If we are hot and cold in this, a deeper journey will prove elusive. God may well test our integrity before he reveals himself to us—so don't give up!

To be serious about pilgrimage is to develop habits involving spiritual practices. You might think having habits and routines (such as prayer lists, for example) is for spiritual babies, but I don't agree. Our goal is to develop something more spontaneous and inner-directed, but habits and routines can help get us there. Let's face it: the prosperity and relative safety Westerners enjoy means for most people there is little driving us to our knees in a desperate hunt for God. Initially, routines or structures can form a frame-work for spiritual practices to position us close enough to God to be stirred by his love and grace. Set practices make it easier to stick with a routine because we don't have to reinvent the wheel each time. So, ironically, we often fail to find deeper spiritual springs, not because we have these structures in place but because at some point, we don't.

Because life is hectic and with many distractions, we must be intentional about finding our own personal "tent of meeting" where we go consistently to meet with God—a place and time allowing us to get away from noise and other people to engage *consistently* in effective spiritual practices, to cry out to God, or just to cry! Do you have such a place? This doesn't need to be for hours, but if we prioritize enough time to be still and to hear God daily it will revolutionize our soul! *Simple engagements with God on a regular basis are the key to building a real relationship with him.* At one point my "tent of meeting" involved escaping to a little lake at dusk when the birds came to feed. After moving away, I rebuilt my "tent of meeting" around walks early in the morning, but this "tent" has been invaded by my young children. We must fight for a meeting place.

Our spiritual practices or exercises *must stretch the boundary lines of our heart and in this way help us to grow into the character of Christ.* If they are too difficult we might give up, but if they are too easy they won't stretch us—by definition they would not be spiritual *exercises.* They must help us exercise our will so that our pride, self-preoccupation, doubts, and worldly perspectives are put to the sword.

To be stretched, we might need to find a practice that helps us move beyond straight Bible reading to meditate on Scripture and look between the lines for *spiritual* insight. Again, perhaps we wholeheartedly embrace the importance of genuine love but now need to find a way of expressing it in practice. The practices themselves should not become the thing we aim for and talk about. The goal is *not* to read the Bible, pray, fast, or meditate more. No. *The goal is God himself.* We must press further by making sure our practices are effective—that they help us hear God in such a way we find the inner energy to respond.

Building Spiritual Momentum

What can we do to position ourselves so God can instruct our hearts? The following suggestions don't form an exhaustive list or a prescriptive formula by any means, but show the kind of spiritual practices that will help to introduce desert dynamics into our spiritual pilgrimage and tap into the flow of God's life.

It is not one-size-fits-all. You must find a blend of practices that offers *you* spiritual traction. The blend will depend on your makeup, your practical circumstances, and your spiritual season. Some years ago, I reconnected with God by spending extended periods of unstructured solitude puttering in my vegetable garden. At the time I was in survival mode, but in hindsight I see this was an appropriate spiritual practice for my spiritual season. It helped me be available to God when I had no energy for spinning any other spiritual wheels. Now I am in a different season. More structured approaches to meditating on Scripture are bearing fruit for me, together with mental or interior prayers—spontaneous *inward* expressions of soul-thoughts and affections as part of an ongoing conversation with God described by Teresa of Avila as "not an act of thinking much, but of loving much." I am also appreciating afresh how memorizing Scripture provides scope for God to speak his truth to me.

Retreating is a time-tested practice that has fresh relevance for increasingly busy societies. When members of our church community struggled to find time to go away on retreat, we have run guided retreats that engage people with God at home for around an hour a day across a week or two.

Other spiritual practices are less contemplative and more practical, such as serving the poor. This is one of eight spiritual practices described by David L. Goetz in *Death by Suburb: How to Keep the Suburbs from Killing Your Soul*. Besides pleasing God, this enriches our souls with a sense of relative prosperity, while spending time only with the well-off can leave us feeling (relatively) poor. The modern classic *Celebration of Discipline: The Path to Spiritual Growth* by Richard Foster is also a rich resource on the topic, as is: *The First Spiritual Exercises*, adapted by Michael Hanson from the writing of St. Ignatius Loyola.[132]

Essential Spiritual Practices for Every Jesus Follower

The following suggestions apply in cathedrals and cafés and across the span of Christian traditions. Their greatest rewards will come from consistent application over time.

1. GRASP YOUR IDENTITY AS "DEARLY LOVED BY GOD"

God our Father and Creator brooded lovingly over the process of our creation in our mother's womb with delight (see Ps. 139:16), anchoring our identity in his vested interest in our wellbeing. The implication of our identity as God's dearly loved children—that good is coming to us and we are invited to intimacy with God as our Father—gives us an adventurous attitude to the spiritual life. Our souls are at rest, ready for instruction, and we can believe our Father will speak with us. *However, when sin in our lives rob us of this security, we entangle our souls in a search for significance through success and other things that create inner noise and make it difficult to hear God.* How do you see your identity in Christ?

God gives his Spirit to enable us to assume our identity as his dearly loved children, to embrace the privilege of intimate conversation with him, and as legitimate candidates for goodness and intimacy, to cry, "*Abba,* Father" (see Gal. 4:4–7).

2. BRING YOUR HEART INTO PLAY

We can be pilgrims out of hunger for intimacy or because our life is shipwrecked, but unless our inward attitude is one of pursuit rather than escape, the spiritual reality of God will be elusive. To find something, we must look for it, and Jesus taught the same is true of finding God (see Matt. 7:7).

If the framework of our Christian lives serves as a check-the-box providing a means of escape instead of a sincere pursuit of God, this becomes a *spiritual* barrier to direct access to the presence of God (see Heb. 9:8).

The apostle Paul saw an attitude of pursuit as a cure for spiritual dullness:

But the people's minds were hardened, and to this day whenever the old covenant is being read, the same veil covers their minds. . . . But whenever someone turns to the Lord, the veil is taken away (2 Cor. 3:14, 16 NLT).

If our hearts are passive on the sidelines, how can the Holy Spirit instruct us? We must at least cry out for the desire. It matters whether we have wide-eyed childish wonder and trusting expectation of God, or remain squinty-eyed and guarded toward him. Would you describe your attitude to God as pursuing or escaping? Why?

3. LEARN TO PRAY

We should keep on asking, looking, and knocking, not because our persistence will mobilize God to act for us, but because Jesus is already acting (see Lk. 11:9–10). *Prayer is a dynamic conversation connecting us relationally with God, who is always at work all around us.*

In 1974 American author Annie Dillard retreated in Virginia's Blue Ridge Mountains where she lived in a little cabin for a year to contemplate creation. Her book *Pilgrim at Tinker Creek,* a contemplative journal of her retreat, won a Pulitzer Prize in 1975. She recognized the beauty dancing around her but also the snarling cruelty and shadows—no superficial abstraction—and after it all gave God a standing ovation. Eugene Petersen described what Dillard was doing as "praying with eyes open"[133]—looking and seeing that "grace is everywhere." God is all around.

On a walk in the beautiful alpine region in Victoria, Australia, I took in the soothing murmur of the river, the subtle layers of light like heavenly mist on the ridges, and the sky's piercing blue. My soul was trying to cope with this assault of wonder when there was a shot of color and delightful sounds as a flock of rainbow lorikeets swooped around me, playfully dipping, turning, and whistling. With senses overloaded, I prayed: "Ohhhhh, Lord!" It was the sort of "speech" exchanged between parent and infant that develops trust—rich in meaning but unimpressive content-wise. It wasn't a detailed exposé of my needs making me feel in control because I covered everything; it connected me with the God who was already all over my needs—like an infant making connection with mom or dad as the answer to everything. Prayer is more the language of intimacy and relationship than information or motivation—not third-person commentary about God or language that makes things happen, but language *to* and *with* God as the speech of love and response.[134]

We don't pray to fight for a piece of grace, but because "grace is everywhere" and by relating to God we join ourselves with the ocean of it everywhere: we experience God all around us. This is why we change, and our circumstances change when we pray. And without seeing this, prayer is boring—akin to persisting at a government office to get paperwork signed off. All religious grind but no true spirituality. Flat. No expectation. But when we ask, look, and knock, all things are in the hands of our Father who withholds harmful things we request out of our foolishness and takes up genuine needs we haven't even recognized. Grace is bouncing all around. Surprises abound. And in and through a life of prayer, God gives us the Holy Spirit—himself (see Lk. 11:11–13).

How would you describe your own prayer life?

4. MAKE TIME TO LISTEN

The world today seems to be in a big hurry, and way back in 1950, A. W. Tozer prophetically recognized the looming issue of time for the spiritual life when he wrote: "The man who would know God must give time to him."[135] Busyness is the archenemy of the spiritual life. Jesus went to the mountainside to listen to his Father (see Lk. 5:16), because it takes time (even for Jesus) to escape the clutter of voices around us to become aware of God's voice. *Making time to listen and respond is a non-negotiable for cultivating correspondence with God.*

To really listen to someone speaking right in front of us is difficult enough, let alone listening for the voice of the Spirit in the spiritual dimension. Reading the Bible for facts takes as long as it takes to read the words, but we must linger and listen between the lines for spiritual knowledge.

Spiritual practices have been developed over time to help us listen to God. One example from the 1500s is the prayer of Examen, developed by St. Ignatius Loyola. Through a simple reflection on the events of the day—at the end of each day or as a morning prayer to review the previous day—it is designed to help us live in God's presence by making us aware of God's gifts and the ways he is working in our lives. Make sure you are comfortable and relaxed and be aware of your breathing, your body, and your feelings. The following five simple steps[136] should take fifteen minutes to complete:

1. Give Thanks: *Allow yourself to become aware that you live in the stream of God's love—where all is gift.* In God's company, review your day, recalling its gifts large and small, and allow gratitude to well up in you.

2. Ask for Help: *Ask the Holy Spirit to bring clarity and understanding to whatever happened.*

3. Review: *Review your day, hour by hour, to see how God is working in your life.* Over time, look for patterns of events or relationships that bring inner peace and enliven your soul or, conversely, things that make your soul feel thin and desolate. Look for the ways God works best in you, and how you work best with God.

4. Respond: *Respond to what you felt or learned in the review of your day.* What is God saying? How has he affirmed you? What sins has he revealed? Do you feel wonder, sadness, or sheer delight with the Lord? Speak with him about it and respond.

5. Resolve: *Consider with hope and God's grace, the loving way forward tomorrow.* Ask the Holy Spirit for help to grow or change, to develop some virtue or gift, to find healing or renewal, and act in response to your new awareness. Do your best and surrender the outcome to God.

5. LEARN HOW TO READ THE BIBLE

The Bible is the source of authority for Jesus-followers, but we must hear what it really says if it is to draw us away from inferior things to God and our sacred life. The technicalities of grammar and the historical issue of context are important, but I want to focus briefly on a less understood factor in reading the Bible—the heart.

First, we will struggle to hear what God is saying if we don't truly want to hear it (see Matt. 5:8), or if we suffer with the immaturity of a four-year-old—that is, we have a limited view of the world but think we know it all and lack the humility to absorb richer insight. The deepest truth may not be found in the literal words of the Bible or what we already know, but when we can read Scripture with God's heart—his overarching love affair with humanity—in mind. For example, Jesus healed a man with a deformed hand on the Sabbath because he read Scripture in a deeper way through the lens of his Father's love (see Mark 3:1-6). He appeared to break the Sabbath law, but instead fulfilled it's heart.

One way to discover this transforming lens of love is to spend time in the Gospels, *encountering* Jesus the Living Word, discovering his character, his heart, and his ways. How do you think your life would change if you spent a weekend with Jesus, and why?

6. KEEP GOD'S MERCY IN VIEW

Immersing ourselves in what God has done for us mobilizes us spiritually (see Rom. 2:4b). I have discovered that moving the hull of a sailboat stationary on the sand is like shifting a stranded whale. However, once the boat is on the water and has some momentum, steering is a breeze. *Getting God's mercy in view gets us moving and responsive to God so he is able to steer or instruct us in a transforming way.* Spiritually we become pliable and receptive as God's mercy frees us to submit to his life-giving authority over our lives.

This is what Paul meant when he wrote:

> Therefore, I urge you, brothers, in view of God's mercy, to offer your bodies as living sacrifices, holy and pleasing to God—this is your true and proper worship. Do not conform to the pattern of this world, but be transformed by the renewing of your mind. Then you will be able to test and approve what God's will is—his good, pleasing and perfect will (Rom. 12:1–2).

For Paul the starting point is grasping something of God's merciful love to free us to regularly offer ourselves to God in response—to hear him, to be loved, and to serve. We also resist being conformed to the pattern of this world, expressing hunger for God by leaning toward the pattern of his kingdom by consistently making choices that are consistent with his heart and the life of Jesus. We "lean" toward God with both our heart and the outward expressions of our lives. *We will become like whatever we lean toward and offer ourselves to.* As we consistently respond in these ways to God we position ourselves, according to Paul, for the Holy Spirit to enlighten and transform us so that we understand and love God's will. Accepting the goodness of divine authority brings further response, opening us to deeper discovery of God's mercy, the process kicks in again, and spiritual momentum builds.

7. LEARN TO MEDITATE ON SCRIPTURE

The psalmist's secret to spiritual life and fruitfulness is to meditate on God's Word day and night, like a tree by a river drinking in its water (see Ps. 1:2–3). Meditation means to ponder or reflect on something in a search for its meaning. Beyond just receiving information, we hold onto the truth like a dog with a bone until we can digest it and thus be encouraged, guided, and changed by it.

In the same way food is held up in our digestive tract to give the body a chance to break it down and extract its nutrients, only through "digesting" God's Word can we truly be instructed by it. *This is because it takes more than communicating information to gain the understanding or insight required to trigger a response.* In this light, consider your own approach to God's Word. The mechanics of meditation are not difficult; if we can worry, we can meditate. The challenge comes in wanting to change and to dig deeper into God's Word.

Studying Scripture is a power-packed spiritual practice bringing heavenly thinking into our mental arena. But here I am talking about lingering to hear the rhythm of truth *between* the lines—to ruminate on Scripture and tune in to the resonance of God's love dancing among the words we read. *Our life with God is shaped in a real way not mainly by outward authority ("the Bible says so in words"), but by an inner witness authenticating Christ and his words as the Holy Spirit enlightens us ("my heart also says so").* We can read the words and stories in the Bible and not be changed, or we can rationalize them away and not act on them, but meditation develops an inner witness that instructs our will and is not so easily ignored.

We might say to ourselves, "Wow, Lord, you actually love *me*," or "Jesus, your heart is so pure and beautiful." As we prayerfully chew on this for the rest of the day, we digest it and are nourished spiritually as the Holy Spirit has opportunity to instruct our hearts. Our soul delights as the flavors of God's Word are extracted by the chewing. Many believers suffer spiritual indigestion and dullness because they are not "eating" properly. This is either because we don't know there is a rhythm between the lines, or because we "eat" on the run.

Too often, we are in the state of heightened awareness called stress. Stress makes us like a deer flexing its muscles to prepare to run from a predator. This is part of the survival mechanism for a deer, but for human beings it means too many demands are being placed on the adrenal gland, and our body starts to break down. It also makes it difficult to pick up the whispers of the Spirit between the lines because this sort of fight-or-flight awareness is focused outwardly and is a complete distraction from what is happening inside us. Simple relaxation exercises can help. For example, try closing your eyes and focusing on just one thing while counting your deep breaths—*in* ("one") *and out* (relax); *in* ("two") *and out* (relax), etc., for one minute.

It also matters whether we want God to show us *his* way, truth, and life, or whether we are simply looking to reinforce our own understanding, priorities, and ways. Reading the Bible as we would a newspaper boosts our store of information or confirm opinions we already hold, but with no advance in our understanding. Alternatively, we could read the Bible as we would a book that at first we don't completely understand because it is better or higher than our previous experience. Our understanding of God deepens because rather than simply reinforce current opinions we possess the humility to digest and be instructed by it. Do you think you read the Bible like a newspaper or a "higher" book?

Lectio Divina is a meditative spiritual practice developed by the desert fathers and mothers to allow God to speak directly to us from the text of Scripture. It involves reading a short passage (no more than 6–8 verses unless it is a story) very slowly and attentively over and over. Each time a simple question helps to delve into the meaning of the text and to hear God. The questions also help us to sidestep filters in our minds screening what we hear on the basis of preconceived ideas, or to avoid challenging messages or those we are not aware we need. *The goal is to really hear God speak, not just ourselves.* Here are the steps:

- Prepare—take five to ten minutes in silence to quiet your heart and invite God to speak.
- Reading 1: *What word or phrase strikes you or elicits some response in you*? If you are in a group share your word or phrase succinctly and without further discussion. (Read the text twice if needed to identify a word or phrase.)
- Reading 2: *In what way is your life touched by this word or phrase—what in my life needs to hear it today?* (Share if you are in a group.)
- Reading 3: *What is God inviting you to do or be through this word, and what do you feel about it?* (Share if you are in a group.)
- Reading 4: Allow silence to rest in God's ability to bring about whatever he is inviting you to do or be.
- Response: *What will it look like for me to faithfully live out what I have heard God say to me?* (Share if you are in a group.)

My friend David Macmillan introduced me to the power of turning the truths of Scripture into prayer. By taking a short passage from the Bible and identifying truth themes and keywords, we empower our prayers by saturating them in truth (see Col. 3:16) *about God*. We want to use truths about God and prayers used by lovers of God in the Scriptures to expand our own ability and language for loving God. When we immerse ourselves in truth *about God*, very soon our hearts will experience being close to his Light because we cannot separate God from the truth that *he is*. We want to "pray in the *first* commandment" before the second— to take Scripture and to use it to adore and minister to God by expressing love to him before we make requests of him. I have found, though, making requests comes much easier—perhaps because we feel satisfied at having covered the things for which we need God's help. *But first-commandment prayers are prayers about God, not prayers about us, and this is what makes them so transforming for our soul.* Isn't it the truth *about God* that gives us hope and joy?

The form of our meditation is less important than whether or not, like the psalmist, we deeply and consistently drink in the living water of God's Word.

8. PRACTICE THANKSGIVING

Spiritually uninspired days are part of the journey, but what should we do on such days? I tend to backtrack to what is simple and effective, and for me that is *thanksgiving* (Ps. 95:2). There is not a lot of heavy lifting with this spiritual practice because it simply connects us with what is good around us.

While a student in Los Angeles, I left my warm apartment on campus, with dinner cooking in the oven, to go for a walk. Trudging along and feeling down over something or other, I met Ray. He was a homeless man who had just found a new pair of shoes in a dumpster. He was on top of the world, thankful for his find, and alive in his spirit. I had so much, but because I couldn't be thankful for it, what I had was stolen from me. Ray was rich; I was poor.

Western society enslaves us in the dungeon of always wanting something else—the abundance we have is taken from our hands and our false sense of poverty insulates us from God's stunning goodness. Thanksgiving lifts our eyes to God in appreciation for what we already have so he can show us his salvation (see Ps. 50:23). What can you be thankful for right now?

9. BE HONEST WITH YOURSELF

A young man struggling with drug addiction promised never to lie to me but misled me in the next breath. The key to his freedom dawned on me. He needed to be honest with *himself*. We can be preoccupied with building an impressive façade for our spiritual progress, but it won't help us much. Being honest with ourselves is critical for spiritual growth because we can only grow from where we truly are, not from where we are pretending to be. Reflect on whether you are honest with yourself.

When Paul wrote that "speaking the truth in love, we will grow to become in every respect the mature body of . . . Christ" (Eph. 4:15), he was saying *acting truthfully* is important for our spiritual growth. To act truthfully is to be open about what is real and true for us in light of our desire to follow Jesus, even if we fall short of the mark. Having honest, open-hearted conversations with others about what is real and true for us helps us to be authentic in our correspondence with God—in a context of love, it is integral to true Christian community. But it is easier to have "elephants in the room" than to be honest. Elephants take up space in our hearts and leave no room for love or the Holy Spirit.

When the undercurrent of our community is love, and we feel safe enough to say, "I feel hurt and angry because of what you did" or "I don't understand" or "I want to find God but can't" or "I have sinned by . . ." or "I feel afraid," we give the Holy Spirit access to instruct and restore us inwardly.[137]

It Doesn't Just Happen

Revolution follows when we are "barefoot," but it doesn't just happen. Spiritual momentum develops as we believe and position ourselves through spiritual practices for God to instruct, or train, our souls. For those of us hungry for God this is core business.

For Discussion

1. Do you think it is significant for your own life with God that our heroes of faith were helped by spiritual enlightenment? Explain.

2. In Romans 2:17–29, what do being "instructed by the Law" and "circumcision of the heart" show us about what it means to be a true Christian? What does it mean to "approve of what is superior"?

3. Discuss this statement: "If our hearts are instructed by the Spirit and we resonate with the *rhythm* of the law, we won't be under the hammer of its *rules*."

4. What did Jesus mean when he taught that eternal life is to know God spiritually? How does this change your approach to life with God?

5. Share a practical issue you face in positioning yourself for the spiritual life.

6. From the practical suggestions for positioning ourselves for heart instruction provided at the end of the chapter, discuss the *one* that you think will be most helpful for you. What concrete things could you do to implement the suggestion?

PART FOUR

Final Briefing for the Revolution

CHAPTER 10

"Purify My Heart!"

Oh how powerful is pure love for Jesus
that is not mixed with self-interest or self-love!

—THOMAS À KEMPIS

W e now confront what is possibly our supreme hindrance to cultivating a life with God and being truly alive—ourselves. A pure heart offers a powerful advantage for realizing a life close to God.

Good Conduits

Jesus said, ". . . my judgment is just, for I seek not to please myself but him who sent me" (John 5:30). Because his soul was not cluttered with self-interest and self-love, his judgments about things flowed from the very mind of the Father. *He was a perfect conduit for God's thoughts because he was holy and his heart was pure.* Saints and psalmists alike made this connection between inward purity and spiritual understanding. Thomas à Kempis reflected Psalm 119:100 when he wrote, "If you were inwardly good and pure, then you would be able to see and understand all things well without obstruction."[138]

The Imperfect Can Be "Pure" Too, Thank God!

We have a much better understanding of the state of our own hearts than we like to admit (see Prov. 14:10). Just a little introspection makes me conscious of ways I put out an inner welcome mat for impurity. What about you? I know when I dillydally with prideful ambition, envy, unforgiveness, doubt, or lust rather than sentencing them to death by my clear intent to pursue the heart of Jesus. I know it when I rationalize to stay the execution of the impurity I harbor, or sabotage the process of transformation by my sluggish cooperation. I know when my conscience is alert enough to register repugnance over the ways in which I differ inwardly from Jesus. And I also know the lightness, freedom, and inspiration of the crisp inward resolve that leads me to cry, "Purify my heart, O God!"

God knows it all too, and while people judge our outward appearance or deeds, he judges our heart or motives. Faith in Christ whisks us to heaven despite our sin, but in the meantime, the purity of our heart sends ripples through our spiritual life. Obviously, *indulging* impurity will be an obstacle to seeing God. But if we *genuinely* desire to be pure, God will graciously overlook our imperfection and allow us to see him as part of our pilgrimage toward holiness. Case in point: the shockingly imperfect people in the Gospels who recognized the Messiah. In this sense, the imperfect can be pure too, thank God! How else will sinful human beings encounter a holy God this side of Christ's return?

Looking Inside Ourselves

Most people are scared stiff of what they might find in a face-off with their true selves. Perhaps we aren't as powerful, loving, knowledgeable, or indispensable as we want to believe. Perhaps we are more hurt and in need of a good cry than we show. Perhaps our faith is brittle; we are angry, harboring secret sinful habits, or have exhausted our spiritual resources. What are you afraid to find? To be whole, we must recognize both our weakness and strength, liability and giftedness, darkness and light.[139] This prepares a place for repentance, healing, and growth—it gets us into the zone where grace happens. *Real spirituality is inward and downward toward what is true about ourselves, not upward and outward to escape the truth or to make up for its deficit.*

We must look inside ourselves because most of our struggles are in *us*. Like pesky weeds, they sprout from the inner impurity or un-holiness of our lives. This can display itself right in the middle of our pain, or when we are mistreated—as when we are slow to forgive, when we wallow in self-pity and resist the love of others so we can be victims or seek revenge. We take a crack at blaming, and, of course, there are injustices in the world. *But, at bedrock, we struggle when we can't find meaning, and therefore joy, doing what we know to be right and good; when we can't see these things as the means of grace in practice.* Our hankering for worldly success is a formidable "enemy within," wreaking havoc upon our souls via energy-sapping complexity and disharmony with the Spirit. Thomas à Kempis wrote, "Whenever we desire anything excessively, we become those who are not yet perfectly dead to themselves, are quickly tempted and overcome in small and unimportant things."[140] Can you think of something you "desire excessively"? Reflect on how this robs you of peace.

This unholiness exhibits itself menacingly through self-seeking: we can find meaning and deep value only in things that feature *us*, that swing the spotlight onto *us*, or that win adulation for *us*. It is the need to spearhead a "happening" church, to be more spiritual than others, to pray more profound prayers, to be more prophetic, and preach or say things that have everyone talking about *us* more. It finds new ways of expression in hardship:

> Self-seeking desires to awaken men's sympathy, can be easily insulted, expects gratitude from people, and does not permit itself to be served. The self-seeking, precious ego takes care that every eye sees, and that every ear hears *him*, "the patient sufferer," and cannot understand why everyone does not have sympathy with him. The very clearest sign of self-seeking is complaint about others.[141]

If you have suffered inner torture because something you are involved in does not showcase *you*, this unholiness has distorted your soul. Self-seeking tempts us to pinch something for ourselves out of ministry or Jesus-allegiance rather than being content to go empty-handed, as Christ did, to serve others for the Father's glory.

Can you grasp how powerfully self-seeking might distort our decision-making and limit our kingdom involvement? How it derails our journey into the life of love?

Inward Fatigue

When we cling to a vision or way of life for a time but don't see the expected outcome, we can experience "inward fatigue." Do you think you are in this boat? King Solomon described it this way: "Hope deferred makes the heart sick, but a longing fulfilled is a tree of life" (Prov. 13:12).

We can stumble into the trap of comparing ourselves with others (see 2 Cor. 10:12). For example, we might hear others confidently say, "God said . . .," while we struggle to hear God's voice. We imagine they have some sort of direct audience with God, and feel like a failure. But most of the time the person was just referring to a hunch or impression in their mind's eye. Besides, is God perhaps doing a deeper thing with us if it is taking longer? We must be encouraged by the fact that God's pie is infinite; even when someone else gets a whopping slice, it has nothing to do with the slice apportioned to us.

At the extreme, this heartsickness manifests as burnout, and we feel helpless, worn out, and unhappy, and everything seems pointless. Church leaders suffer burnout in staggering numbers. But any of us unable to rise above the demands of our ego and the importance of our own success will experience diminished joy— and the key to following Jesus is to find it within ourselves to do so consistently *with joy*! When what we are doing is chock-full of meaning because we realize it is somehow integral to what God is doing, we will find joy and fulfillment in doing it whether or not the results are flashy.

To avoid inward fatigue, we have two choices: adjust our expectations of the kingdom or our personal expectations of success. Something must give. We can be tempted to neglect hidden soul-work to fast-track what we see as our spiritual progress. Leaders disillusioned by the dullness of their congregations might be tempted to lubricate the cogs of church machinery to make things "work." Those biblically defined expectations of disciples we have discussed in this book are sidelined as idealistic goals too difficult to realize. We must adjust our personal expectations about our own success.

True Love's First Kiss

At the end of the blockbuster movie *Shrek,* the title character kisses Fiona, but she remains an ogre and cries, "I don't understand. I'm supposed to be beautiful." Shrek replies, "But you *are* beautiful." True love's first kiss (or experiencing God's love) frees us to accept ourselves the way God has fashioned us. The world (and sadly also the church) tells us to pursue *success* in something we haven't yet achieved, resulting in an endless treadmill of trying to be more beautiful, important, or noticed.

The temptations of Jesus, immediately on the heels of the Father's expression of love at his baptism, rattle his cage to test how deeply the Father's love is shaping his soul. *He is being tempted away from wholeness to the treadmill of establishing his significance by being successful.*

As Henri Nouwen saw it, in the desert Jesus was tempted to be relevant, spectacular, and powerful.[142] In needing to be *relevant*—to turn stones into bread—we try to do things, show things, prove things, and build things. We are too busy serving ourselves to live and work prayerfully, or to be contemplative. We engage in a flurry of activity, but our correspondence with God is sparse. Being *spectacular*—throwing ourselves down from the temple—is about winning acceptance and rising to stardom by presuming upon God. Popularity elevates us above others, but we all (including leaders) struggle with sin and are broken people who need healing, care, and love. What we do for God is something, but we all need to forgive and to be forgiven, to know and be known, to teach and be taught. Finally, Jesus was tempted to be *powerful*, and for us this means trading the purity of our worship to clutch at our own kingdom. It is to fudge on God's Word to secure honor, position, and power for ourselves, and to spiritualize it into the bargain.

What does the way you are in your skin tell you about your experience of God's love?

Richard Rohr, in *Everything Belongs*, makes the point: our struggle to live in the fullness of the present moment siphons away our happiness. The secret to being happy, he says, is to learn to realize everything is here right now—the present moment is as perfect as it can be, and, therefore, to let it be full and sufficient. The space we occupy right now is not as empty as it might appear to be or that we fear it might be because God is in it with us like a runner ready to explode from the blocks to express his love. For this reason, our pain, failure, and frustration can belong in the present.

Our tendency is to try to control or transform the present moment. We treat it as if it doesn't belong and try to fix, change, manipulate, control everybody and everything, complete things, blame, criticize, prove, perform, and work overtime to be noticed. Can you identify some ways you try to do this? *If we are not in the present moment with everything that it means right now, God can't be in it with us.* If we are busy creating a different or better moment, we can't correspond with God here and now.

Seek First the Kingdom

The antidote for inward fatigue is to take a *spiritual* rest—a vacation for the soul from performing and worrying and pleasing people, to let God love us. Spiritual rest is a moratorium on anxiously fussing to get results (even spiritual results) and to rigorously shake free of the unsanctified expectations from ourselves and others we have allowed to wriggle into our souls. It clears the mind for sacred whispers of love telling us we are beautiful and significant even if the wheels have fallen off our wagon, and we are far from where we want to be or where others expect us to be. *It is to accept our identity and worth from God rather than from our achievements or the accolades of people.* What things stop you from taking a spiritual rest?

In his Sermon on the Mount Jesus called us to spiritual rest by being carefree like the birds and lilies (see Matt. 6:25–34). They don't anxiously fuss about not having a worm to eat or a place in the sun, nor do they scheme to get more; they simply get on with things and enjoy what is provided because the Father is at work throughout his creation. He is always caring, even for birds and flowers, so we should trust that he will care for us, too, and simply keep our eyes on him and his kingdom.

It was written of Thomas Merton that, "He began to see that the highest spiritual development was to be 'ordinary,' to be fully a man, in the way few human beings succeed in becoming so simply and naturally themselves . . . what [people] might be if society didn't distort them with greed or ambition or lust or desperate want."[143] It is the grace to respond to God rather than to worldly compulsions. Do you feel this freedom, or are the influences of the world bringing turmoil to your soul?

Impurity loitering in our hearts, in whatever form, renders our spiritual lives adolescent. But if we are aware of it, hungry enough for God and honest enough with ourselves, we are well on the way to countering it. And this we must do if we are to get down to the business of marching to the beat of Christ's drum. Other helpful practices are the focus of our last chapter.

For Discussion

1. Discuss the connection between inward purity and spiritual understanding in the context of the statement of Jesus in John 5:30.

2. Apart from the work of Jesus on the cross, how can the imperfect be pure? Why is this important for the spiritual life?

3. Why is it important to look inside ourselves? Try to share one thing you notice when you consider the true condition of your own heart.

4. What is "inward fatigue," and what are the contributing factors? To avoid it, should we adjust our expectations of the kingdom, or our personal expectations of success? Why?

5. Discuss this statement: "When we let God love us, we become *whole* in the sense of the rest and peace of being happy in our skin." What does this have to do with the spiritual life?

6. If we are trying to control or change the present moment, how does this impact our correspondence with God?

7. Discuss the idea of spiritual rest as Jesus described it in Matthew 6:25–34, and the challenges you face in taking such a rest. How is that rest an antidote for "inward fatigue"?

CHAPTER 11

Staking a Claim

If a man does not keep pace with his companion,
perhaps it is because he hears a different drummer.
Let him step to the music which he hears.

ON THE GRAVESTONE OF EDMUND BANFIELD,
AKA "THE BEACHCOMBER,"
DUNK ISLAND, AUSTRALIA

We are more prone to perform religiously for God's love than to freely receive it, to adore ourselves rather than God, and to seek our own good rather than that of others. Following Jesus into the life of love does not come naturally—we must stake a claim for it, like pioneers staking a claim on new, undiscovered land.

The Spiritual Chrysalis

Having said that, the reality of sin means if we are to consistently follow Jesus into the life of love, our hearts must change. It's not just a matter of finding a technique or model to help us circumvent faulty soul-circuitry so we can do what is right; we commit to a *process* of change by the Holy Spirit. This takes place within the dynamic kingdom rhythm of the life of love—the inward journey of discovering God's love and the outward journey of expressing it to others and restoring our world.

These inward and outward journeys together form a spiritual version of a chrysalis, the transitional stage between caterpillar and butterfly where development and metamorphosis occur. The difference is that, unlike a caterpillar in a chrysalis, we are not passive.

Thankfully, God's part is to do the changing; it is all grace. But as in any relationship, we must play our part, and our part is to involve ourselves consistently in the inward and outward journeys as the basis for a spiritual chrysalis. How committed do you feel about engaging in these journeys?

Any Way into the Sphere of Love Will Do

God always loves us first, and while I believe the discovery of God's love is the primary requirement for life with God, it doesn't end there. It's more a case of *continuing* to stake claims to God's life of love by involving ourselves in receiving his love, and expressing love to him and others, in an ongoing way. Our sense of God's love might be "thin," but enough to want to plumb its depth and height or to express it practically. We might be impatient in prayer or toddlers when it comes to spiritual practices. Some of us discover God's love through suffering and pain while others might discover it through a seemingly uninspired commitment to reading the Bible. *Any way into the sphere of love will do to provide God with opportunities to reveal his love, change our hearts, and work through us.* The important thing is to stake claims, in one way or another, inside the rhythm of the life of love.

For example, we might pursue the spiritual life so the Holy Spirit can show us more of God's love (a stake). As we do this, we are learning how to love and are making choices to this end by sharing the gospel, praying for someone, or serving in a practical way (another stake). We will both fail and experience joy while learning about ourselves and getting our hands into the sweetness of God's mercy from the giving end. We might be convicted of an area of sin in our lives and experience liberating forgiveness (one more stake). As we hear his words and his love expands the horizons of our soul we find new and greater freedom to express God's love in practical ways (yet another stake). From where you are now, can you think of some achievable ways you could drive some stakes into the life of love?

The point is simple: we keep immersing ourselves in the sweetness of God's mercy and goodness from both the receiving end and the giving end. *As we march to this beat, we find ourselves transported to the place of spiritual metamorphosis because the beat has gently guided us to involve ourselves with the Creator.* The opportunity itself is deep grace.

For the pioneers to remain on their land, they needed to be able to live in the wilderness where they would start their new lives, no matter the inherent dangers or their lack of experience. In the same way, staking our claims to the life of love is just the start, and we must grow to be able to sustain everyday life there. *If we continually drive stakes into the ground of this new God-life, the land becomes ours by virtue of the fact that we are involved with God and that he graciously prepares us for the life we have claimed with our stakes.* Have you been disappointed trying to fly spiritually before you have had a robust spiritual life in place? Because we cannot change ourselves, our immediate goal is not butterfly but chrysalis—it is Christ and his beat. Without this perspective, we will soon pack up our wagons and head back to the familiar.

Cassie's Story

When Cassie joined our church community in her late teens, she was in-and-out of the hospital battling severe anorexia nervosa and depression. On one visit to the adult psych ward she knelt and apologized to God for shutting him out for so long; she was scared and she needed him.

Cassie learned she could hear God's voice, and started to find revelations that set her free, step by step. She felt God speaking to her about *choice*, and this changed her thinking that was distorted by the eating disorder. She says, "The words from God painted my world an entirely different color." She began to love finding truths from God that set her free, staking claims to God's kingdom here and now. As she walked closely with God in this way—hearing him and responding instead of drowning in hopelessness—she found freedom from her debilitating darkness and torment.

As I write, Cassie has been recovered for ten years, is married, and given birth to her first child. She says, "I can feel God interacting with me in new ways all the time." When the darkness lifted, she began to identify again with her childhood passion to help the poor overseas and has trained as a nurse so that God can bless the world through her.

Eight Practices to Help Us Stake a Claim

Remember that most of the pioneers were ordinary folk who faced a sharp learning curve. And certain things helped them in their quest. For example, if they were clear about the land they wanted to claim, they were less likely to hesitate and find that others had beaten them to it. Equally helpful were provisions and skills for the journey, along with savvy about natural sources for food and water for when their initial supplies ran out. They needed to be mentally prepared for times when the whole thing felt mostly wild and rarely wonderful.

In the same way, certain practices (we will discuss eight of them below) will help us as we seek to stake a claim to the life of love Jesus demonstrated—a life that is both wonderful and wild. These practices should not be seen through the eyes of a manager who masters techniques to make him effective in a short time. Rather, they should be embraced with the humble heart of a farmer who is dependent on the divine instruction woven into nature. He humbly prepares fertile soil and dynamics conducive to the growth of a crop by forces that are beyond him. The manager strives; the farmer is a non-anxious presence as he faithfully prepares the soil, tends it, and humbly waits.

1. CALL FOR THE BALL

In football or soccer, the main game happens around the ball. You truly join the game when your wholehearted cry is, "Pass it to me!" A less confident soccer player might think, *I hope that ball goes somewhere else!* We can balk in the same way at the seminal facets of Christ's life of love, or at doing "inner work." Perhaps we lack the self-confidence for it or feel our own needs (often byproducts of our desperate lunge for prosperity or success) sapping our desire. Perhaps we simply misunderstand the implications for the spiritual life of *not* calling for the ball.

Rather than contend for prayerful mountainside rendezvous with the Father, opportunities to witness or pray for the sick, or soul-stretching opportunities to love, we are content for those balls to pass us by. Often we don't even get on the field—with the poor, sick, and lost; with downtime in our diary to be available for God; or inside ourselves where impurity and pain are entrenched and "inner work" is needed—for fear the ball will come to us. And it won't. *If we want the ball, we must get on the field.* Practically speaking, in what ways are you on the field?

We think if we mount cogent excuses for not wanting the ball, they will somehow neutralize the spiritual fallout. But no matter how hard we convince ourselves that just filling space in an obscure position on the field is the main game, the action is still around the ball. Vital life with God will always pivot around a dynamic spiritual and love-saturated correspondence with him, and excusing ourselves will smash us spiritually.

With clarity about wanting to play the game, football players call for the ball, and spiritual pilgrims are "barefoot"—ready, engaged, learning, risking, immersed in the game up to their eyeballs.

2. DISCOVER FOR YOURSELF

Until you discover the truth for yourself, *you* will have no knowledge of it. For example, if someone merely describes an insanely delicious dessert, it might pique your interest, but once you taste it, you will salivate and your hunger will drive you until you can savor it again. *In the same way, self-discovery brings spiritual hunger and momentum.*

You might blindly believe something about God or because an influential person believes it, but this is not enough to render you "barefoot" and ready to follow and correspond. Writer and educator Parker Palmer shows that the accepted model of knowing truth is inconsistent with the way we come to know things in real life.[144] This is presented graphically in figure 4.

PARKER'S COMMUNITY OF TRUTH

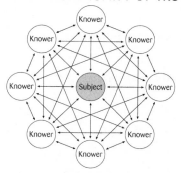

FIGURE 4

In the dominant model of truth-knowing, truth (a set of propositions about objects we cannot have relationship with) flows down from the top via experts who are qualified to know truth, to amateurs who are qualified only to receive it. Subjective thoughts can't flow back up because they might tamper with the neat propositions. *Amateurs are not invited to discover truth; they are told what it is.* This assumes the propositions will become truth to the amateurs simply in the telling.

Alternatively, in Parker's "community of truth," there is a subject at the center of the community—for Christian communities this is Christ—and subjects are available for relationship. We have the very real task of keeping Christ Center and Subject rather than some removed sort of object. *Everyone can discover the Subject themselves and be a firsthand knower of truth.* This does not mean everyone can have their own *version* of truth, but to encounter God's truth in Christ is the only way it becomes truth *for us*.

When people are invited to discover truth for themselves, they might find the process becomes complicated and, possibly, uncomfortable.

> As we try to understand the subject in the community of truth, we enter into complex patterns of communication—sharing observations and interpretations, correcting and complementing each other, torn by conflict in this moment and joined by consensus in the next. The community of truth, far from being linear and static and hierarchical, is circular, interactive and dynamic.[145]

However, it is in this interaction and interdependence that the Holy Spirit works powerfully to instruct the heart because this is what happens when people are finding things out for themselves. It is a *creative* chaos because we are engaging again and again around Christ, and if you seek, you will find. What challenges and opportunities does this idea of creative chaos raise for you?

We must connect some dots. We should look at sermons and books as drawing a part of the circle and inviting us into an open space where we can complete it by adding *our own* insights, hearing what the Spirit is saying to *us*, and making personal application in *our* lives.[146]

We must resist the temptation to want ready-made answers and instead welcome good, open questions because answers are only true for us if somehow *we* find them. When I started asking open questions during sermons and allowing time for people to contribute, the space was nervous and thin. The gap and the silence were threatening. However, as people realized their contributions were respected and wanted, the interaction became fervent and enriching. An incomplete circle creates a liminal space where we are drawn from our comfort zones and face challenge and danger. It stretches us, and this is the only way we will grow and find new meaning.

Importantly, this is when we discover not only how we are relating to our world or to God, but what is going on inside ourselves to cause these responses. *Informed by God's love, fresh responses that would make our souls dance the tango come onto our radar.*

When our church engaged in a deeper search for Christ, some of us struggled because we only knew how to relate to Jesus as an object. Some were understandably afraid to opt out of the false security of propositional faith (knowing all the answers), and to admit to having questions. For others, this was just too much hard work. It is difficult to appreciate nature, the textures of music and art, or the wonder of God's love as concepts taught by others: such higher things must be approached in the deepest sense of personal encounter. Think about ways you could do more discovery work for yourself.

3. COMMIT TO A JESUS-COMMUNITY

The coals of a fire burn hotter and longer when they are together than when they are in isolation. The same is true spiritually. Being integrated into a community of passionate pilgrims fuels our own pilgrimage.

The Greek word *koinonia* (fellowship; "participating together in" something) was used to describe the first Christian communities.

What made these fellowships distinct from the many trade guilds and Jewish and Gentile religious groups in the ancient world was this: they participated together in *Christ*, not a vocation, or a love for lattes for that matter. They were radical because Jews and Gentiles, slave and free, men and women related to each other on equal terms.[147] *There was spiritual leverage in the communities because the members were participating together in Jesus—they let him define them as a group, and this manifested in a radical, hostility-smashing love.*

The spiritual power of true Jesus-community burrowed into my understanding at the memorial service for an elderly auntie. The proceedings were tediously religious at times, but that didn't matter—my auntie and her grieving friends had shared faith together. *They'd had a common fellowship with Jesus over time.* And as these grieving friends belted out hymns together, the hopeful refrains sung by their fellows in front and beside, without faltering, fortified their souls. Grace flooded back into everywhere.

Jesus-community is fertile soil for the spiritual life because it shapes what is normal. For example, it reinforces the belief that listening into the ether to hear an unseen God is faith, not fantasy. Community esteem for the Bible as God's Word and the encouragement of other believers encourages us to reject popular worldly ideas and ways for kingdom thinking in everything. In community, prayer and love are kept central. Submitting to the initiatives of others in worship is good for the ego—it gets us used to the idea we aren't God. And a confessing community helps us see that failure is normal, enabling us to keep corresponding with God as sinners rather than abandon ship because we can't be perfect.[148]

Relationships with Jesus-people offer unique opportunities to test-drive and deepen dynamic correspondence with God: as they express God's love we receive it, and vice versa. Through the use of spiritual gifts God uses people to heal, grow, love, and speak to us. We gain confidence hearing God's voice when someone else hears it too, and we have a safe environment as a test pad for our leadings. Again, God's grace filters into our souls when someone accepts or forgives us, cheers our aptitude for something, supports our vision, or keeps us accountable. Others on the journey can sharpen our self-awareness when we delude ourselves.

4. BUILD STRUCTURES TO SUPPORT A DYNAMIC CORRESPONDENCE WITH GOD

Vulnerable seedlings don't "take" without the support of a stake. In the same way, we can develop structure in our lives to give a dynamic correspondence with God a chance to "take" and deepen.

Peppered throughout church history are examples of structured little fellowships with the dual aim of supporting an inward journey of spiritual transformation and an outward journey of serving others—and they harnessed the power of community to do it. In the 1700s, John Wesley started supportive fellowships called *Class Meetings* that embodied inward and outward journeys by reflecting his rules for moral living: (1) do no harm or any kind of evil; (2) "do all the good you can, by all the means you can, in all the ways you can, in all the places you can, at all the times you can, to all the people you can, as long as ever you can"; and (3) do the ordinances of God or the things by which we have communion with God (such as daily worship and prayer, and study and meditation on Scripture). Wesley sought a balance between piety and acts of service as a means of grace or finding God's life, and group members kept each other accountable for it.

Many small groups I have led would have ventured into much deeper spiritual terrain if they had used a structure that intentionally supported the basic rhythm of life with God. How well have your small groups achieved this? To live with God, a dynamic correspondence must "take" beyond Sundays. A weekly dab at physical exercise won't get you very far, and ditto for the spiritual life.

In our church community, Restore[3] small groups (God's *restoring* mercy, grace, and love to the power of three) provide support and accountability for people in their attempts to live out both sides of our paradox—receiving God's love and expressing it to others. Restore[3] groups are based around Mark 3:14–15, where Jesus appointed the Twelve specifically to *Be with him*—the transforming discovery of God and his love (inward journey) and *Be sent*—for Spirit-empowered kingdom life and ministry (outward journey). The Restore[3] groups (which can also form the basis for informal fellowships) encourage and support the basic rhythm of a dynamic correspondence with God until it "takes." They are power-packed because they involve people with God, but also because of the synergy of three (or more) keen "pioneers" intentionally exploring the frontier of God's love together, and working together prayerfully to plan and then to express God's mercy, grace, and love in the world in an accountable context.

The groups meet weekly at any time or place that is convenient to do two things:

(1) *Engage in inward spiritual practices*—the "inward" part of the journey aimed at developing intimacy with God and receiving insight and love from him through *worship using songs* (to sing *to* God rather than *about* God; as we bless him with our worship we too are blessed), *prayer* (either silent prayer embracing the presence of God and his action in us, or declaring wonderful truth about God and asking for his help in our pilgrimage), and *reflection together* on pre-read Scripture or other material (i.e., with a simple focus on the life and teaching of Jesus, the kingdom, or the spiritual life). Each member then tells the group how they feel God is calling them to respond in the following week, and they will be made accountable at the start of the next group meeting.

(2) *Express God's mercy, grace, and love to restore our world*—to train ourselves in the "outward" rhythm of the spiritual life by intentionally expressing mercy, grace, and love *to the least, and those searching for God.* As the Holy Spirit prompts, the group will plan projects[149] together during group time; implementation will be outside the group meeting. One group member might know someone who is searching for God and needs practical help or the ministry of the Holy Spirit to heal her, and the others would join him in that expression of God's heart. Collaboration helps those who are shy or fearful and harnesses creative juices, faith, and gifts—to the power of (at least) three.

The key elements of a Restore³ group take forty-five to sixty minutes, and if the members are *very* focused, the group meeting could be squeezed into thirty minutes during a lunch break at work or school. The key goal is to utilize relationships to help us get an in-out rhythm in place, but other elements—such as extended fellowship or ministry—can be added around it if time allows.

Whether the group involves focused study of the Bible or less formal reflection on it, the goal of the Restore³ group is to answer the question, "What are you saying to *me*, Father?" Also, as we seek to practice the inward and outward rhythms of the life of Jesus, we ask not only, "Do you know this?" but, "Are you consistently living this out?" To start a group you simply need to find two others who are not content with their spiritual status quo.

5. DEVELOP THOSE BASIC SKILLS FOR THE SPIRITUAL LIFE

Many Christians wrongly assume they have the basic skills and practices for life with God under their belt. We get a rude awakening. Practicing the basics can seem boring, but in the wilderness the basics can mean life or death. Skills—such as the ones described in detail throughout this book—including reading the Bible, prayer, and hearing God's voice, aren't automatically in our toolbox at sign-up. When church meetings are nothing but wall-to-wall words, contemplation and spiritual alertness can be lost. Thankfully, we can learn to pray, journal, and meditate—the kind of skills allowing us to do work on the inside where we find freedom and become "barefoot." Which skills do you feel you need to develop?

Because disciples are made, not born, we must be trained in the skills and practices for the journey toward God. Training takes us from being theorists full of head knowledge to practitioners who can *do* the kingdom life. Bring on good teaching, but the kingdom life is more caught than taught. The goal is to be able to do it on our own.

This was the great assignment Jesus left for his disciples: to *train* people in his way of life, and in the practice of all he had commanded them to do (see Matt. 28:19–20). He strategized for spontaneous expansion from a *natural system*. By "natural," I mean its life happens organically, freely, or by natural instinct, rather than under the control of something. We sight the expansive effect he envisioned in the way fractals work. Fractals are the self-similar patterns that spontaneously repeat themselves in a relentlessly expanding way to form clouds, mountains, many plants, and our brains (see figure 5 below).

A SPONTANEOUSLY EXPANDING FRACTAL

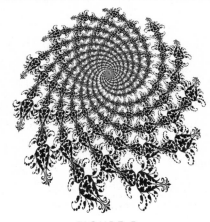

FIGURE 5

Atoms and molecules relate freely, in a seemingly chaotic way, but they engage again and again around a few simple principles as if divinely instructed. *Christ's strategy hinged on followers having the love-fueled inner energy and practical skills to engage again and again around the simple kingdom principles and practices he taught.* This dynamic sparks spontaneous and expansive kingdom advance in fractal fashion.

In recent decades, the church has suffered a spiritual-skills drain. Professionals do it all, so the rest have no need for these skills, and this leaves us dead in the water spiritually. Discipleship develops the skills required for the trip.

6. DO WHAT YOU BELIEVE

Until we put Christ's words into practice, believing them is pointless—something that comes home to roost when we struggle to weather the storms of life (see Lk. 6:46–49).

Today we seem preoccupied with debating doctrine to find truth, but unless we follow the *way* of Jesus, his life will remain elusive (see John 14:6). For example, knowing the concept of love is one thing, but by actually loving we touch something of God, and its sweetness tinkers in liberating ways with our heart DNA. Make a list of things Jesus taught that you believe to be true, and note which ones you do or don't actually do.

The early followers had hearts on fire well after Pentecost— because of the baptism of the Holy Spirit, yes, but they were also deeply committed to putting the Christian life into practice (see Acts 2:42–47). The Holy Spirit doesn't supplant Christian practice, but to the contrary, provides divine inward impetus for it.

Roland Allen, a missionary in China from 1895–1903, showed that because new Christian converts were not allowed to express their godly zeal, the church was not experiencing spontaneous expansion.[150] While Muslim converts in Africa were allowed to teach, new

Christian converts were sidelined to get their doctrine up to scratch. This gag on expressing their faith caused their zeal to die away.

If we always hanker for heady celestial revelations, we can be distracted from doing the simple things we already know and believe. Thinking we are doing something because we believe it doesn't count. An honest audit helps. Start simple and small but with committed consistency, and remember: *beginning gets you halfway toward the goal.*

7. ACT LIKE AN ADULT

We are more likely to find God if we decide to grow up before we grow old, because the trek into the spiritual wild is all about our will—deciding, responding, taking responsibility and initiative in faith. My six-year-old would always act like a six-year-old if I treated her that way by doing everything for her. We suspend ourselves in a perpetual state of spiritual infancy by assuming it is more natural for us to be apathetic, to avoid responsibility, and to be told what to do because we can't discern it for ourselves. But, of course, this diminishes the work of the Holy Spirit as our resident Helper.[151] What assumptions do you hold here?

We abandon our infancy when we understand we get to make a free choice to listen and obey, or to thumb our noses at what Jesus says. The consequences for what we do with our time, our money, our bodies, our minds, and our hearts are in our hands.

8. GET YOUR DEFINITION OF THE CHURCH STRAIGHT

If we are merely playacting the life of love, we aren't the church. My definition of the church is not new, but it differs from the way many believers define it: *the church consists of communities of people who have been liberated by God's love in Christ to live their daily lives immersed in God's presence and for his pleasure.* We ravish his heart with adoration and become Spirit-empowered conduits for his love to flow into the world. How does this fit with your own definition or practice?

The church exists for what God has called it to do—to join him in restoring all of creation. The kingdom of God (his rule and reign) comes to the world through the church as an instrument for salvation, mercy, acceptance, love, justice, reconciliation, healing, friendship, practical help, freedom, provision, comfort, forgiveness, and peace as God's love compels us (2 Cor. 5:14–15). These grace-filled responses of individuals to God's love together form a mosaic of God's magnificence, drawing others to worship and march joyfully to the beat of Christ's drum as he blesses the world for his Father's glory. *When we realize just showing up doesn't make us part of the church, staking a claim for Christ's new life takes on fresh meaning.*

I imagine when the early church in Jerusalem met in their homes (see Acts 2:46),[152] there was a defining *in*flow from their involvement with God since they last met; the larger gatherings at Solomon's Colonnade were the same (see Acts 5:12). *The point is that God's life was already flowing from "out there" (in the everyday lives of rank-and-file believers) to "in here" (the gathering).* This added spiritual spice and power to the meetings. It is what Paul meant in 1 Corinthians 14:26, where he described some of their local church meetings as being more like a spiritual potluck. Their gatherings weren't supposed to be free-for-alls for pet agendas or theological hobby horses. No. Everybody brought something received from God "out there" to the meeting "in here," and God manifested himself in and through the tapestry of the combined contributions for his redemptive pleasure and glory.

We slaughter this dynamic today by reversing the "flow," and this is like reverse thrusters for the spiritual life. Sunday meetings run by "experts" are used to catalyze some sort of desire for involvement with God (in mainly inert spectators) that will flow from "in here" to the "out there" of our everyday lives. If the meeting is good enough, persuasive enough, or provides enough supernatural evidence God is real, then there may be some response for a time "out there," but this is soon forgotten and the onus returns to the meeting to convince us again. How dependent are you on the church meeting for your God-involvement?

Important debates abound about the *form* (size and structure) of the local church, but a truer measure of the spiritual vitality of a church community involves the direction of the *flow*—whether believers are bringing anything to contribute to its spiritual life because they are immersed in God "out there" in the everyday—stories of God at work, faith for healing or provision, a song of praise, love, a word of encouragement, witness, a prophecy, a heart softened by repentance, revelation from God's Word, vision, creative ideas for advancing the kingdom, and resources for it. What do you contribute *spiritually* to your faith community?

The grace we receive from our everyday journey of corresponding with God would flow *into* the gathering like a spiritual pick-me-up. *God* is front and center. Anticipation is high that he is on the job as we each come as a participant in the kingdom to receive and to be used by God.

Are You Ready?

The Bible is a relentless invitation to a spiritual life with God—to an inward revolution of grace enlivening our souls that spills out redemptively into our outside lives and broken world. But that won't happen without dogged perseverance.

The invitation beckons us inward to the heart, to the mystical, and to knowing things spiritually about God by which we are ready for him, willing—"barefoot." We must courageously trek into the life of love like salmon swimming upstream, cultivate a dynamic correspondence with God as a way of being, and develop the skills required for it. We might be fighting our way clear of spiritual dullness or shaking free of dogged unholiness in the lower decks of our souls, and all the while acquiescing to shifts in our will as we find grace for it. No quick fixes here, but isn't it worth all the effort? Should we expect less to share in the divine life?

In Papua New Guinea, our family traveled to outlying islands in an open aluminum dinghy powered by an outboard motor. On a day etched in my memory, we faced an angry sea with a menacing swell randomly gathering to form dangerous peaks up to fifteen feet high. I was in my mid-teens and on "reef watch," sitting at the front of the dinghy with my legs dangling over the bow. As we hurtled down the face of a rolling swell, a peak formed in front of us like a blue monster. Dad yelled, "Hold on!" Plunging into the fifteen-foot wall of seawater, Dad wrestled the arm of the outboard motor and again yelled, "Hold!" The motor gurgled eerily as its exhaust was submerged. With seawater up to my waist, again the rallying cry came: "Hold!" After seemingly forever, the dinghy punched through the monster's belly. The motor let out a high-pitched wail, and we recovered to tackle the next swell.

In the same way, life and the spiritual journey will take us on a collision course with "blue monsters"—problems too big, amorphous realities, testing disappointments, roads too long and rough, impossible spiritual challenges, pain too deep, egos too vigorous, time too short, God too distant. But true pilgrims don't balk. Instead, girded by the relentless call of the Scriptures, they faithfully build spiritual momentum in their lives to the pilgrim's rallying cry: "Hold!" They keep at it until, in the mystery of things, they punch through to grace and God.

If you hear the rhythm and beat of a different Drummer, my prayer is that you will have the courage to step to the music you hear—to listen to your heart and take up your calling. To do what you can't *not* do, and to ask, "Is the life I am living the same as the life that wants to live in me?" To stake claims to it by living by the Bible rather than your experience until the two are united. To dare to act on the outside in a way that honors the truth you hold deeply on the inside, and to "Hold!"

God calls us to a revolution of love for his pleasure and glory just as he called Moses—not with a test of natural abilities or know-how, but with a test of the heart. Are you ready? It begins here: "Take off your sandals, for the place where you are standing is holy ground."

For Discussion

1. In what ways does following Jesus into the life of love not come naturally to you?

2. Discuss the idea of a "spiritual chrysalis." What is your part, and how are you fulfilling it?

3. Discuss this statement: "Any way into the sphere of love will do to provide God with opportunities to reveal his love, change our hearts, and work through us."

4. How does Cassie's story inspire or challenge you?

5. Are you more likely to see the kind of practices that help us stake a claim to life with God through the eyes of a farmer or a manager? Which approach is more fruitful and why?

6. Share which of the eight suggested practices for staking a claim to life with God captured your interest and explain how you will apply them to your life.

7. Discuss the story about the dinghy and the importance of "holding" for the spiritual life. What "blue monsters" are you facing on your spiritual journey?

Acknowledgments

I am grateful to my fellow travelers at Foothills Church, who are courageously embracing change for a deeper life with God, and in this way have contributed to this book.

I acknowledge the invaluable contributions of feedback and encouragement at different times from: Bec Marshall, Doug Yoder, Dave Macmillan, Derek Morphew, Graham Twelftree, Don and Annette Marshall, Kirrilee Trist, Robert Gallagher, Mark Fields, Costa Mitchell, Thom Gardner, Peter Marshall, Samuel Mitchell, Rob Norman, Russ Cooke, Jim Hart, Zillah Williams, Kathi Macias, Phil Fox Rose, Jon Sweeney, and Robert Edmonson.

Thank you, John David Kudrick, for being more than a wonderful first-up editor but also a champion of my message in a way that was game-changing for me.

Notes

INTRODUCTION

1   A. W. Tozer, *The Divine Conquest* (Carlisle, Cumbria, UK: OM Publishing, 1993), 21–24.

CHAPTER 1

2   Jack Hayford, "How God Evaluates Worship." *Leadership Journal* (Spring 1999): 29.
3   Rom. 1:7, 7:14–25.
4   Dallas Willard, *Knowing Christ Today* (New York: HarperCollins, 2009), 19.
5   For other times when people removed their shoes in the Bible see Joshua 5–6 and John 13:1–17.
6   Oswald Chambers, *My Utmost for his Highest* (Grand Rapids, MI: Discovery House, 1963), 109. See Ps. 34:7.
7   Parker J. Palmer, *The Courage to Teach* (San Francisco: Jossey-Bass, 1998), 112–113.
8   Exodus 18. The number forty signifies preparation in Scripture (see Gen. 7:4; Ex. 24:18, 16:35; Josh. 14:7; Ezek. 29:11,12; Jonah 3:4; Matt. 4:2; Acts 1:3). The spiritual development of Moses was evident in his character and faith responses, as seen for example in Exodus 14:5–14.
9   C. B. Keogh, ed., *Readings for Mental Health* (Sydney, Australia: GROW Publications, 1975), 9.
10   For a good glimpse at mystical theology, read St. Teresa of Avila, *Interior Castle* (New York: Doubleday, 1989).
11   For example: Isa. 44:3; Ezek. 47; Dan. 2:44–45; Joel 3:18 and Zech. 14:7–8.
12   See Mark 3:14–15, Matt. 28:18–20, and Paul's teaching on spiritual gifts (e.g., 1 Cor. 12).

CHAPTER 2

13   G. Steinberger, *In the Footprints of the Lamb* (Minneapolis, MN: Bethany House Publishers, 1936), 11.
14   Joel B. Green, *The Gospel of Luke* (Grand Rapids, MI: Eerdmans, 1997), 430–431.
15   Hannah Whitall Smith, *The Christian's Secret of a Happy Life* (Peabody, MA: Hendrickson, 2004), 159.
16   Religion today is riddled with the idea that we must remove what is not good in us to be worthy of God's love.
17   This is made possible by the incarnation, death, and resurrection of Jesus.
18   Michael Hansen, S.J., *The First Spiritual Exercises: Four Guided Retreats* (Notre Dame, IN: Ave Maria Press, 2013), 8. See John 14:25–27 and Philippians 4:4–7.
19   Thomas à Kempis, *The Imitation of Christ* (North Brunswick, NJ: Bridge-Logos, 1999), 119.
20   Kempis, *The Imitation of Christ*, 127.
21   Luke's consistent concern in the lead-up to when Jesus visits the sisters is with genuinely hearing the word of God and doing it. This is the point of the parable of the sower (see Lk. 8:4–15), after which Jesus says, "My mother and my brothers are all those who hear God's word and obey it" (Lk. 8:21 NLT). Immediately before Jesus visits the sisters, he tells the "Parable of the Good Samaritan," who is distinguished from the priest and Levite as an exemplar of the greatest commandments because he heard the word *and did it*.
22   The apostle Paul taught the Galatians to refrain from trying to earn God's love, but they *were* to make choices for what was other than the desires of their sinful nature (see Gal. 5:13).
23   Dallas Willard, *The Great Omission* (Oxford, UK: Lion Hudson, 2006), 61.

24   Baptism is a public enactment through immersion in water (a biblical symbol for the Spirit and life of God) of an ongoing commitment to this sort of life.

25   Thomas Merton, *The Wisdom of the Desert* (Boston, MA: Shambhala, 1960), 7–8.

26   Ibid.

27   At the lowest level of consciousness we are self-focused instinctively for survival, then: find meaning and identity conforming to our tribe or group; self emerges and lives for itself; we perceive an all-powerful Other with rules we must follow to prosper; we manipulate the natural laws of our rational world for our gain (modernism); truth becomes relative, we are skeptical about life based solely on money, status, and power, and pursue answers to deeper questions of life (postmodernism); a discovery of our powerlessness; and, finally, the discovery of a more complete reality (or God) making others and their well-being integral to our full existence.

28   Green, *The Gospel of Luke*, 471.

29   Merton, *The Wisdom of the Desert*, 19.

30   Biblically *shalom* is about wholeness—the relational restoration (with God and others), true peace, order, security, prosperity, harmony, and abundance that would be experienced across the creation if by the presence of God the wholeness experienced in Eden were restored.

31   Gordon D. Fee, *The First Epistle to the Corinthians* (Grand Rapids, MI: Eerdmans, 1987), 633. Jesus also taught that doing great things for God, even miracles, gains us nothing in terms of intimacy with Christ if we are simply using him to make ourselves look important (Matt. 7:21–23). Again, without expressing the Father's will through genuine love, we forego an opportunity to be united with God by sharing his essential nature.

32   The main source for this story and the quotations that follow here is James Gilchrist Lawson, *Deeper Experiences of Famous Christians* (Anderson, IN: Warner Press, 1970), 83–91.

33   Kenneth Scott Latourette, *A History of Christianity, Volume I: Beginnings to 1500* rev. ed. (San Francisco: HarperCollins, 1975), 221.

34   The church embraced the idea if you confessed and repented of your sin and did the required "penance"—good works to show sorrow for sin—you would be absolved or forgiven by the priest. Indulgences could be purchased from the church instead of doing such penance.

35   F. E. Stoeffler, *German Pietism During the Eighteenth Century* (Leiden, Netherlands: E. J. Brill, 1973), 8.

36   J. I. Packer, *Concise Theology: A Guide to Historic Christian Beliefs* (Wheaton, IL: Tyndale, 1993), 178.

37   Some were hyper-spiritual, like the Corinthians, and emphasized the promptings of the Holy Spirit but ignored God's Word. Others embraced the gnostic idea that only the soul gets saved, so what we do with our bodies is inconsequential, or believers are seen as sinless because they are in Christ and so their actions are immaterial as long as they believe.

38   Melvin E. Deiter in *Five Views on Sanctification* (Grand Rapids, MI: Zondervan, 1987), 15.

39   The seeker-sensitive movement, for example, has focused on making the church more palatable to unbelievers but, in the process, has paraphrased the gospel to suit busy prosperous Westerners who need their emotional needs met but don't have time for discipleship or the spiritual life.

40   Like Montanism in the latter part of the second century, greater power was given to prophecies from the *pneumatikoi* or "spiritual ones" than to the teaching of the New Testament. As with the Corinthians, they waited for a "word" from God rather than responding in practical obedience to the clear teaching of Jesus and the apostles.

CHAPTER 3

41 Project Gutenberg; A. W. Tozer *The Pursuit of God,* available as an e-book from Project Gutenberg. www.gutenberg.org

42 Rick Joyner and Robert Burnell, *The Harvest Trilogy* (Charlotte, NC: Morningstar Publications, 1989), 39–64.

43 Mark 1:15.

44 Henri J. M. Nouwen, *The Way of the Heart* (New York: Ballantine Books, 1981), 15.

45 Ibid., 25.

46 Benedicta Ward, *The Sayings of the Desert Fathers* (Kalamazoo, MI: Cistercian Publications, 1984), 3.

47 One of the conclusions of a believer and an atheist who attended twelve churches across America and recorded their personal, subjective experiences in Jim Henderson and Matt Casper, *Jim and Casper Go to Church* (Carol Stream, IL: Tyndale House, 2007).

48 The basis for this, is the teaching in the Bible that God desires to transform us to become like his Son Jesus (2 Cor. 3:18). The point of the teaching of Jesus in the Sermon on the Mount in Matthew 5 is that the good life that God promises is experienced by us as we grow to become different sorts of people—people like Jesus. This is why Jesus, full of the love of the Father, calls us to follow him and learn of him (Matt. 11:28–30).

49 Hansen, *The First Spiritual Exercises,* 12.

50 Colin Marshall and Tony Payne, *The Trellis and the Vine,* (Kingsford, NSW, Australia: Matthias Media, 2009), 123.

51 Ibid.

CHAPTER 4

52 See Mark 7:20–23; Galatians 5:19–21; Jeremiah 17:9; 1 John 1:10.

53 John R. W. Stott, *The Message of the Sermon on the Mount* (Leicester, England: IVP, 1978), 40–41. (Consider: Would Jesus say that someone suffering bereavement is well off because they will be consoled at a later time?)

54 To see God face-to-face is called the "beatific vision," or the vision that makes us blessed or happy. See also: 1 Corinthians 13:12 and Revelation 22:3–4.

55 Leon Morris, *The Gospel According to Matthew* (Grand Rapids, MI: Eerdmans, 1992), 101.

56 1 Peter 4:15–16.

57 Matthew 10:1–8, 28:18–20; Luke 9:1–2, 10:1–20.

58 The Bible is consistent in making the state of the heart the criteria for participation in God's life (Matt. 15:17–20, 23:26; Prov. 4:23; and 1 Sam. 16:7).

59 See John 15:26; Ephesians 4:18–19.

60 Richard Rohr, *Adam's Return* (New York: Crossroad, 2004), xi–xii.

61 Eugene H. Petersen, *The Jesus Way: A Conversation in Following Jesus* (London, England: Hodder & Stoughton, 2007), 82.

62 Rohr, *Adam's Return,* 31–32.

63 Rohr, *Adam's Return,* chapter 14: "Jesus' Five Messages," 155ff.

CHAPTER 5

64 The ultimate blessing is being close to God, or "seeing" him (Ps. 17:15). The "beatific vision" refers to the perfect happiness anticipated when we see God face-to-face (see 1 John 3:3; 1 Cor. 13:12). This anticipated happiness comes from knowing what God knows, and who God really is—his love, power, and grace. St. Cyprian, a Bishop of Carthage in the third century, described it as "delighting in the joy of immortality."

65 Jesus taught that corresponding dynamically with him is the essence of discipleship by which we discover truth and freedom (John 8:31–32). His hearers blindly claimed that being related to Abraham by blood was enough for a life-giving relationship with God (John 8:33–47). Jesus recognized their blood-tie with Abraham but pointed out that this failed to bring them the life of God because they were not corresponding dynamically with God as Abraham did.

66 This is what King David meant when he said, "Because of my integrity you uphold me and set me in your presence forever" (Ps. 41:12).

67   Leanne Payne, *The Healing Presence* (Grand Rapids, MI: Baker Books, 1996), 53.

68   For an explanation of these keys that will help you apply them to your own life read Mark and Patti Virkler, *4 Keys to Hearing God's Voice* (Shippensburg, PA: Destiny Image, 2010).

69   See John 5:19 and Ruth Haley Barton, *Pursuing God's Will Together: A Discernment Practice for Leadership Groups* (Downers Grove, IL: IVP, 2012).

70   Virkler and Virkler, *4 Keys to Hearing God's Voice,* chapter 4.

71   Hannah Whitall Smith, *The Christian's Secret of a Happy Life*, 99–107.

72   To learn more about *consolation* and *desolation* in the context of discernment see Haley Barton, *Pursuing God's Will Together*, 57–61.

73   Haley Barton, *Pursuing God's Will Together*, 188–196.

74   Virkler and Virkler, *4 Keys to Hearing God's Voice, chapter 5.*

75   For example, King David was favored by God despite the fact that he failed morally, because he remained responsive to God even in failure (Ps. 51). Jesus incensed the Pharisees precisely because he advocated responsiveness over against their religious attempts at moral perfection (e.g., Lk. 11:37–54).

76   Kempis, *The Imitation of Christ,* 131.

77   Steinberger, *In the Footprints of the Lamb,* 17.

78   Romans 5:12–14 is clear that Adam and Eve's sin applied to all human creatures.

79   Dallas Willard, *Renovation of the Heart* (Leicester, UK: InterVarsity Press, 2002), 112.

80   Eugene H. Petersen, *The Contemplative Pastor: Returning to the Art of Spiritual Direction* (Grand Rapids, MI: Eerdmans Publishing, 1989), 118–121.

81   I discovered this term in Jim Henderson and Matt Casper's *Jim and Casper Go to Church* (Carol Stream, IL: Tyndale House, 2007).

82   John Wesley, *Forty-Four Sermons* (London: The Epworth Press, 1944), 11–19.

83   John Wesley, *Forty-Four Sermons,* 14–15.

84   See Deuteronomy 23:20; Matthew 25:27.

85   Eduard Lohse, "Rabbi" in *Theological Dictionary of the New Testament*, vol. 6 (Grand Rapids, MI: Eerdmans, 1969), 962.

CHAPTER 6

86   For an incisive discussion of this question, read Parker J. Palmer's excellent book *Let Your Life Speak* (San Francisco: Jossey-Bass, 2000).

87   The insights from Gordon Cosby that follow were expressed in an interview with him at Baylor University. See http://www.baylor.edu/content/services/document.php/145343.pdf.

88   See for example Luke 9:12–17 and Mark 8:14–21.

89   Because of the joy set before him, Jesus endured the cross (Heb. 12:2).

90   R. H. Strachan in Leon Morris, *The Gospel According to John* (Grand Rapids, MI: Eerdmans, 1971), 674.

91   For example, see Luke 7:36–50, 23:39–43, 23:50–56; Mark 7:24–30; and John 19:38–42.

92   Eugene H. Petersen, *A Long Obedience in the Same Direction* (Downers Grove, IL: IVP, 1980) is a helpful and practical guide to what it means to correspond with God using the Songs of Ascents.

93   Jesus can see a Samaritan as an exemplar of the greatest commandments (Lk. 10:25–37); the one discerning leper who returned to offer his allegiance was also a Samaritan (Lk. 17:11–19). Samaritans received the message of the kingdom through the ministry of Philip (Acts 8:5–26).

94   Other examples of normal conventions include: a commitment to the welfare of "you and yours" to the exclusion of others; overworking as a means of securing the future; and defining success in terms of external, self-focused markers rather than love, peace, and kingdom fruitfulness.

95   See for example Luke 5:33 and 7:33.

96   Green, *The Gospel of Luke,* 440.

97   Morris, *The Gospel According to Matthew,* 144.

98 Jesus taught that following him might involve challenges to our primary allegiance to our family of origin (Lk. 8:19–21, 12:49–53; Acts 4:32–5:11).

99 This was an aspect of the sending of both the Twelve (Lk. 9:3) and the seventy-two (Lk. 10:4).

100 For helpful insights into the place of forgiveness in the inner healing process read: Thom Gardner, *Healing the Wounded Heart* (Shippensburg, PA: Destiny Image, 2005), 75–77. Gardner's effective model for inner healing identifies the following lies as the main focus of the devil's work: fear, rejection, worthlessness, shame, insecurity, defilement and hopelessness.

101 See Luke 22:39–46. The Apostle Paul taught that we should fight against the strategies and tricks of the devil using God's armor (Eph.6:10–18).

102 Richard Rohr, *What do you mean...FALLING UPWARD?* (a DVD produced by: Centre for Action and Contemplation, PO Box 12464, ABQ, NM 87195; www. cacradicalgrace.org)

103 For us this attitude can extend to the promise of our own resurrection (1 Thess. 4:13–18).

104 Whitall Smith, *The Christian's Secret of a Happy Life*, 148–149.

CHAPTER 7

105 "Satisfied with Blindness," written by Terry Talbot. Used by permission.

106 Andrew McDonough, *Webster The Preacher Duck* (Unley, SA, Australia: Lost Sheep Resources Pty Ltd, 2007).

107 J. I. Packer, *Concise Theology: A Guide to Historic Christian Beliefs*, 157.

108 The main source for the story is Omer Englebert, *St. Francis of Assisi: A Biography* (Ann Arbor, MI: Servant Books, 1979).

109 Englebert, *St. Francis of Assisi: A Biography*, 27.

110 William L. Lane, *The Gospel of Mark* (Grand Rapids, MI: Eerdmans, 1974), 158.

111 Morris, *The Gospel According to John*, 205–206.

112 Spartacus was a folk hero who led a slave uprising against the Roman Republic in 73–71 BC.

113 For this reason, Jesus denounced the cities in which he performed most of his miracles (Matt.11:20–24).

114 Both Jesus (Matt. 7:21–23) and Paul (addressing immaturity among the hyper-spiritual Corinthians) refute the notion that if God works through us supernaturally, we are *necessarily* mature.

115 Ward, *The Sayings of the Desert Fathers*, 5.

CHAPTER 8

116 The exact source is unknown. Perhaps it is misquoted from the British poet and satirist Samuel Butler (1612–1680) who wrote: "He that complies against his will is of his own opinion still."

117 Morris, *The Gospel According to John*, 405–406.

118 Mortimer J. Adler and Charles Van Doren, *How to Read a Book* (New York: Simon & Schuster, 1972), 5.

119 See Mark 8:34–36; John 14:6.

120 St. Teresa of Avila, *Interior Castle* (New York: Doubleday, 1989), 104ff.

121 James Thwaites, *Renegotiating the Church Contract* (Cumbria, UK: Paternoster Press, 2001), 37–45.

122 Ibid., 43.

123 People seek a corporate identity to be part of something bigger than themselves. The dull believer demands something seen because they can't discern what is bigger but unseen (2 Cor. 4:16).

124 Thomas L. Friedman, "The Humiliation Factor." *The New York Times* (November 9, 2003). http://www.nytimes.com/2003/11/09/opinion/the-humiliation-factor.html

125   After Thomas touched the wounds of Jesus and believed, Jesus said that even better blessings were in store for those who believe (who see spiritually) *without* seeing physically (John 20:29).

126   John C. Lai, *Andragogy of the Oppressed: Emancipatory Education for Christian Adults,* The Fielding Institute—HOD Program (Abstracted in *Resources in Education,* Nov. 1996).

CHAPTER 9

127   See Proverbs 2:1–11.

128   J. Alec Motyer, *The Message of James* (Leicester, England: IVP, 1985), 70.

129   In John 14:23, Jesus does not mean "Obey and you get my presence," but, "If you welcome my rhythm of love by being loved yourselves, obeying will come naturally, and you will live in my presence."

130   Morris, *The Gospel According to John,* 720.

131   In "Becoming Like Christ," an article by Richard Foster sourced from www.renovare.org.

132   Details for sourcing these three books: David L. Goetz, *Death by Suburb: How to Keep the Suburbs from Killing Your Soul* (New York, NY: HarperCollins, 2007); Richard Foster, *Celebration of Discipline: The Path to Spiritual Growth* (New York, NY: Harper & Row, 1988); Michael Hanson, S.J.,*The First Spiritual Exercises* (Notre Dame, IN: Ave Maria Press, 2013).

133   Eugene H. Petersen, *The Contemplative Pastor: Returning to the Art of Spiritual Direction,* 67–85.

134   Petersen, *The Contemplative Pastor,* 90–94.

135   Tozer, *The Divine Conquest,* 20.

136   Adapted from Hansen, *The First Spiritual Exercises,* 148–149.

137   In Ephesians 4:25–27, Paul makes this point using anger as an example.

CHAPTER 10

138   Kempis, *The Imitation of Christ,* 81.

139   Palmer, *Let Your Life Speak,* 70.

140   Kempis, *The Imitation of Christ,* 26.

141   Steinberger, *In the Footprints of the Lamb,* 50; the whole book exquisitely describes the holy life of the Lamb.

142   Henri J. M. Nouwen, *In the Name of Jesus—Reflections on Christian Leadership* (New York: Crossroads, 1999).

143   Monica Furlong, *Merton: A Biography* (San Francisco: Harper & Row, 1980), xviii.

CHAPTER 11

144   Palmer, *The Courage to Teach,* 99-106

145   Ibid., 103.

146   See Palmer, *The Courage to Teach,* 120–132, for a helpful discussion on "Teaching from the Microcosm."

147   Robert J. Banks, *Paul's Idea of Community: The Early House Churches in their Cultural Setting* (Peabody, MA: Hendrickson Publishers, 1994), 109–117.

148   Henry Cloud and John Townsend, *How People Grow: What the Bible Reveals About Personal Growth* (Grand Rapids, MI: Zondervan Publishing, 2001), 168–169.

149   Each group member might prayerfully select one other person in the church as their focus for expressions of love as well as participating in a group project to reach people beyond the walls of the church community.

150   Roland Allen, *The Spontaneous Expansion of the Church: And the Causes Which Hinder It* (Grand Rapids, MI: Eerdmans, 1962).

151   See for example: Galatians 5:17–18; 1 John 3:9; John 16:13; and 2 Corinthians 5:16–17.

152   See Banks, *Paul's Idea of Community,* 26–36, for a discussion of the early church practice of meeting in households.

About Paraclete Press

WHO WE ARE

As the publishing arm of the Community of Jesus, Paraclete Press presents a full expression of Christian belief and practice—from Catholic to Evangelical, from Protestant to Orthodox, reflecting the ecumenical charism of the Community and its dedication to sacred music, the fine arts, and the written word. We publish books, recordings, sheet music, and DVDs that nourish the vibrant life of the church and its people.

WHAT WE ARE DOING

Books

PARACLETE PRESS BOOKS show the richness and depth of what it means to be Christian. While Benedictine spirituality is at the heart of who we are and all that we do, our books reflect the Christian experience across many cultures, time periods, and houses of worship.

We have many series, including *Paraclete Essentials; Paraclete Fiction; Paraclete Giants;* and the new *The Essentials of...,* devoted to Christian classics. Others include *Voices from the Monastery* (men and women monastics writing about living a spiritual life today), *Active Prayer,* the award-winning *Paraclete Poetry,* and new for young readers: *The Pope's Cat.* We also specialize in gift books for children on the occasions of Baptism and First Communion, as well as other important times in a child's life, and books that bring creativity and liveliness to any adult spiritual life.

The MOUNT TABOR BOOKS series focuses on the arts and literature as well as liturgical worship and spirituality; it was created in conjunction with the Mount Tabor Ecumenical Centre for Art and Spirituality in Barga, Italy.

Music

The PARACLETE RECORDINGS label represents the internationally acclaimed choir *Gloriæ Dei Cantores,* the *Gloriæ Dei Cantores* scholas, and the other instrumental artists of the *Arts Empowering Life Foundation.*

Paraclete Press is the exclusive North American distributor for the Gregorian chant recordings from St. Peter's Abbey in Solesmes, France. Paraclete also carries all of the Solesmes chant publications for Mass and the Divine Office, as well as their academic research publications.

In addition, PARACLETE PRESS SHEET MUSIC publishes the work of today's finest composers of sacred choral music, annually reviewing over 1,000 works and releasing between 40 and 60 works for both choir and organ.

Video

Our DVDs offer spiritual help, healing, and biblical guidance for a broad range of life issues including grief and loss, marriage, forgiveness, facing death, understanding suicide, bullying, addictions, Alzheimer's, and Christian formation.

Learn more about us at our website:
www.paracletepress.com or phone us toll-free at 1.800.451.5006

 SCAN TO READ MORE

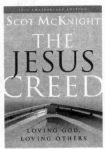

The Jesus Creed:
10th Anniversary Edition
Scot McKnight

ISBN 978-1-61261-578-3 | $15.99 Paperback

With more than 50,000 copies sold, The Jesus Creed teaches you how to live out Jesus's command to love God and to love your neighbor as yourself. When an expert in the law asked Jesus for the greatest commandment, Jesus responded with the Shema, the ancient Jewish creed that commands Israel to love God with heart, soul, mind, and strength. But the next part of Jesus's answer would change the course of history. Jesus amended the Shema, giving his followers a new creed for life, the Jesus Creed: loving God with heart, soul, mind, and strength, but also loving others as themselves.

In *The Jesus Creed: Loving God, Loving Others*, biblical scholar and popular teacher Scot McKnight presents a 30-chapter guide to spiritual formation, rich in theological insight and alive with practical applications.

"Make sure this new guide for living is on your shelf." —Max Lucado

"Scot McKnight brings us into conversation with Jesus in the places and conditions in which we live our ordinary lives." —Eugene Peterson

"[Scot McKnight] has been a kind of secret weapon for my own education and growth. Now he can be yours as well. This book will bring Jesus's world and yours much closer together." —John Ortberg

Fresh Air:
The Holy Spirit for an Inspired Life
Jack Levison

ISBN 978-1-61261-068-9 | $15.99 Paperback

In the Bible, the Holy Spirit staggers us with its unexpectedness. The Holy Spirit is not just about speaking in tongues, spiritual gifts, or "fruits"—but also about our deepest breath and our highest human aspirations.

Provocative and life-changing, Fresh Air combines moving personal anecdotes, rich biblical studies, and practical strategies for experiencing the daily presence of the Holy Spirit. In brief chapters, the book finds the presence of the Holy Spirit where we least expect it—in human breathing, in social transformation, in community, in hostile situations, and in serious learning. Fresh Air will unsettle and invigorate readers poised for a fresh experience of an ancient, confusing topic.

"Fresh Air is, well, a breath of fresh air. Jack Levison invites the entire Christian community, regardless of label, to embrace God's Spirit in the everyday ordinariness of life."—Eugene Peterson

"Jack Levison's book is the most biblical, wide-ranging, innovative, and refreshing book on the Holy Spirit in years."—Scot McKnight

"Levison attests to the quotidian reality of the Spirit in the actual lives of women and men. A subtext of his book is that 'mainline' church folk have a lot to learn from Pentecostals. Fresh Air invites a reread of scripture and re-notice of our own lives in the power of the Spirit."—Walter Brueggemann